A PLU

52 WAYS TO CHEAT AT POKER

ALLAN ZOLA KRONZEK is a professional magician, writer, and educator. He is the author of the *New York Times* bestseller *The Sorcerer's Companion: A Guide to the Magical World of Harry Potter* (Broadway Books, cowritten with his daughter, Elizabeth) and the acclaimed *A Book of Magic for Young Magicians: The Secrets of Alkazar.* He performs and lectures on the history of conjuring at schools, colleges, libraries, and museums. He was a student of magician and gambling expert Frank Garcia.

52 WAYS TO CHEAT AT POKER

HOW TO SPOT THEM, FOIL THEM, AND DEFEND YOURSELF AGAINST THEM

ALLAN ZOLA KRONZEK

Illustrated by Tony Dunn

A PLUME BOOK

PLUME
Published by the Penguin Group
Penguin Group (USA) Inc., 375 Hudson Street, New York, New York 10014, U.S.A.
• Penguin Group (Canada), 90 Eglinton Avenue East, Suite 700, Toronto, Ontario,
Canada M4P 2Y3 (a division of Pearson Penguin Canada Inc.) • Penguin Books
Ltd., 80 Strand, London WC2R 0RL, England • Penguin Ireland, 25 St. Stephen's
Green, Dublin 2, Ireland (a division of Penguin Books Ltd.) • Penguin Group
(Australia), 250 Camberwell Road, Camberwell, Victoria 3124, Australia
(a division of Pearson Australia Group Pty. Ltd.) • Penguin Books India Pvt. Ltd.,
11 Community Centre, Panchsheel Park, New Delhi – 110 017, India • Penguin
Group (NZ), 67 Apollo Drive, Rosedale, North Shore 0632, New Zealand (a
division of Pearson New Zealand Ltd.) • Penguin Books (South Africa) (Pty.) Ltd.,
24 Sturdee Avenue, Rosebank, Johannesburg 2196, South Africa

Penguin Books Ltd., Registered Offices: 80 Strand, London WC2R 0RL, England

First published by Plume, a member of Penguin Group (USA) Inc.

First Printing, April 2008
10 9 8 7 6 5 4 3 2 1

Illustrations by Tony Dunn

 REGISTERED TRADEMARK—MARCA REGISTRADA

LIBRARY OF CONGRESS CATALOGING-IN-PUBLICATION DATA

Kronzek, Allan Zola.
  52 ways to cheat at poker : how to spot them, foil them, and defend yourself
against them / Allan Zola Kronzek.
     p.   cm.
  ISBN 978-0-452-28911-6
  1. Cardsharping.   2. Poker.   I. Title.   II. Title: Fifty-two ways to cheat at poker.
  GV1247.K88   2008
795.412—dc22   2007032935

Printed in the United States of America
Set in Sabon

Acknowledgments

Many people have helped me with this project. For the depth of his insights as well as the breadth of his knowledge, I am indebted to Steve Forte, cheating-scholar extraordinaire and grandmaster of gambling sleight of hand. George Joseph, another superb card handler, charming writer, and casino consultant, was kind enough to share his expertise while finishing up his own book on the subject of poker cheating. Thanks to Jason England, a wizard with words and cards, for acting as technical advisor and passing along numerous insights and examples that found their way into this book. Bob Rosenberger, a collector of antique gambling and cheating apparatus, was very helpful with dates and details about the cheating supply business of yore, and book dealer John Greget got me started with a well-chosen reading list.

Thanks to Regina Cherry for taking the photos on which Tony Dunn, a fellow conjuror, based his drawings. Vaughn and Elizabeth Svendsen provided scientific and literary expertise, and Nick Tarr had wise words about poker as a sacred institution. A tip of the hat, also, to the late Frank Garcia, a superb magician and cheating-detection expert who first showed me how to handle a deck of cards.

A very special thanks to Bibi Wein for a thorough reading of the manuscript, numerous insights, and wise counsel.

Finally, I owe my deepest gratitude to Ruby Jackson for her encouragement, cheerleading, hawk-eyed proofreading, back rubs, love, and humor.

Contents

Introduction

Most people who are cheated at poker have no idea they've been swindled, and those who suspect it rarely have any idea how to think about it. They may have heard of marked cards, but beyond that they have no concept of the range of diabolical scams that can be perpetrated on the unsuspecting player. Consider *52 Ways* a crash course in *how* to think about it: stay with me and you'll learn what can be done, how it's done, and in many cases, how to do it.

Is this unethical? Immoral? Will the secrets within these pages spawn a plague of cheaters? Well, the skinny is here, there's no denying that. The high-jumping trickster brain got busy on card cheating about five minutes after cards were invented in the late-fifteenth century, and hasn't stopped thinking about it since. The legacy is a 600-year-old trail of moves, methods, scams, and subterfuges devoted solely to solving one problem: how to sit down at the table with your fellow card players and steal their money without appearing to do anything out of the ordinary. And that, I should say right off, is what interests me in the subject; not the stealing or the money, but the *methods*, the illusion making, the false appearances, the psychology of deception, and all the multiple layers of reality that go on at the poker table whenever cheats ply their invisible trade.

My perspective is that of a sleight-of-hand magician, not a card thief. This puts me—or, more accurately, I put myself—in very good company. Nearly all of the card-cheating exposés of the past two centuries have been penned by professional magicians: Robert-Houdin in France (1861), John Nevil Maskelyne in England (1894), and in the United States, John Scarne (1933), Frank Garcia (1962), and Darwin Ortiz (1986). While most of these maestros positioned their work as a defense against the dark arts of sharpers, I have little doubt they were initially drawn to the gambling underworld by the keen desire to pry loose the secrets of *exactly* what the card cheats were doing. The truth is that in terms of methodological sophistication, technical sleight of hand, and other tricks of the deceiver's trade, the cheats have always been ahead of the conjurors. Motivated by avarice more than art, card cheats invented bottom dealing, second dealing, false cuts, false shuffles, card switches, deck switches, and stacking procedures; they worked out invisible card-marking systems, invented ingenious codes, and discovered cunning ways of secretly gathering and transmitting information. And perhaps most impressively, they figured out how to get away with their deceptions at close range, more or less in plain view of the audience—their fellow card players. All of this dedicated creativity in the service of robbery is as fascinating as it is reprehensible, and is well worth knowing about, especially if you play cards for money.

As for the ethics of revealing the secrets, the fact is that knowledge alone does not a card cheat make. Also needed are enormous cojones, a willingness to put life and reputation on the line, and the total absence of conscience or scruples. Those who already possess these attributes, it seems to me, need no help from me in getting started. On the other hand, knowledge of methods is the only real way to *defend* against card cheats. It's not foolproof— the most imaginative cheaters are always a step ahead—but it's the best defense there is, other than not playing at all.

About the 52 Ways

Actually there are more than 52 ways to cheat at poker, but nearly all of them are designed to give the cheat one of two advantages: either knowing what cards the opponents hold or will receive, or second, having better cards than they do. Each chapter focuses on a single cheating concept along with variations and applications. Moves and methods, no matter how clever, are useless unless done at the right time and in the appropriate context. Following the explanations are suggestions for preventing or detecting the scam under discussion. Many subterfuges can be defeated by enforcing a few basic rules. Others can be discovered only in retrospect (if at all).

The Principles of Deception

Although the technical work of card cheats and conjurors differs greatly—the methods evolved to achieve different goals—the underlying principles are the same. The deceiver shows the false and hides the real. Showing the false involves simulation, lying, and pretense. For example, the cheat convinces us that he has cut the deck by perfectly *imitating* all of the familiar actions of a cut; however, the deck remains in the original order. Hiding the real involves strategies such as masking (blocking the view), camouflage, and distracting attention. Other essential elements, really a subset of the broader categories, are timing, justification of behavior (providing apparent motivation for the necessary moves), and a deep psychological understanding of what will and will not register with observers. When these strategies succeed—as they do most of the time—the deception is successful and an illusion is created. For a conjuror, the desired illusion is that something extraordinary has occurred. This is known in magical parlance as "the effect." For the cheat the desired illusion is that nothing out of the ordinary has occurred; the effect is that of "luck." The magician and the card cheat are both performers, but only the magician tells you you're watching a show.

The Typical Cheat

It would be ideal if there was a stereotypical cheat to avoid. Not so. Cheats comes in all sizes, genders, and levels of sophistication, and they cheat for different reasons: greed, debt, thrills, and so on. Most try not to call attention to themselves. They handle cards in an unexceptional way and don't seem to win many pots, except for the large ones. Some work alone, or "single-o." Professionals who cheat for a living almost always work in teams. Teamwork opens up a universe of scams that can't be pulled off by one person alone, and makes it far easier to carry out core cheating essentials such as stacking the deck, culling cards, switching decks, distracting attention, and overcoming the cut. Some cheats are specialists and will use the same method—marked cards or peeking, for example—again and again. A mechanic (sleight of hand expert) will employ a large repertoire of interrelated techniques, such as culling, stacking, and false shuffling. Professional cheating crews infiltrate high-stakes games or will sometimes target a single wealthy individual. Amateurs can be found wherever poker is played. The most successful professional cheats are almost always top-notch poker players.

A Little History

52 Ways is not a history of cheating or poker, but historical references appear throughout the book. Here's a brief overview.

One of the earliest detailed accounts of card cheating methods comes from Girolamo Cardano (1501–1576), the great Milanese mathematician and founder of probability theory. An inveterate gambler, Cardano—whose pleasing surname is pure coincidence—describes several types of marked cards, bottom dealing, collusion, stacking the deck, memorizing the order of cards, and the use of a mirror concealed in a finger ring to identify cards as they are dealt. All of this knowledge Signore Cardano apparently earned the hard way, while losing significant lire playing primero, a precursor to poker.

Meanwhile, in Elizabethan England professional card sharps were to be found hustling in bars and taverns, bowling alleys, resorts, and gentlemen's clubs where they passed themselves off as wealthy businessmen. Gilbert Walker (in *A Manifest Detection of the Most Vile and Detestable Use of Diceplay, and Other Practices Like the Same,* 1552) and Robert Green (*A Notable Discoverage of Cozenage,* 1591) describe a teeming underworld populated by a fraternity of pickpockets, thieves, card sharps, and con men. In the company of these assorted swindlers, card cheats were at the pinnacle of the social scale (at the bottom were the *crossbiters* who relied on prostitutes to lure their victims). Says Walker, "They have such a sleight in sorting and shuffling of the Cards that play at what game ye will, all is lost aforehand."

The first American exposé of card cheating, and the first book to mention poker at length, is Jonathan Green's *Exposure of the Arts and Miseries of Gambling* (1843). At the time of publication, cheating at poker was already the rule rather than the exception. By mid-century an estimated 2,000 card sharps were prospering aboard the palatial, floating saloons that were the Mississippi riverboats. Gambling was the preferred way to pass the time, especially among the male passengers, and the ever-changing supply of gullible and wealthy patrons made for a cheater's paradise. When the railroads and the rush for California gold opened the west, card sharps were in the vanguard, setting up shop in frontier towns and mining camps.

By 1880, cheating had become so widespread that virtually every supplier of cards, poker tables, chips, and other legitimate gambling equipment—Will & Finck in San Francisco, Mason & Co. in Chicago, E. M. Grandin in New York, and later K. C. Card Co. in Kansas City—also stocked, advertised, demonstrated, and sold cheating paraphernalia, euphemistically known as "advantage tools." Popular items included holdout machines for switching cards in and out of play, card trimmers and corner rounders for altering the shape of cards, "poker rings" for pricking cards so that they could be identified by feel, and marked cards in every major brand. Much of the business was mail order, and the top cheating houses promoted their catalogues in popular men's journals such as the lurid *Police Gazette*. Any red-blooded American who visited his local barber shop and waited his turn with a magazine was likely to come into contact with an invitation to cheat.

The turn of the twentieth century saw the publication of the first great textbook on card sharping, *The Expert at the Card Table* (1902) by S. W. Erdnase, a graceful writer about whom we know virtually nothing.* *The Expert* differed from all books that came before it. Rather than vilifying card sharping, it celebrates technical sleight of hand as it applies to both cheating and conjuring. Erdnase teaches dozens of advanced card techniques, many of them original. The moves are described in meticulous detail and considered from an artistic as well as a practical point of

---

*S. W. Erdnase is believed to be an anagram for "Andrews," but which Andrews remains a mystery. Recent scholarship has turned up these anagrammatically attractive candidates: M. F. Andrews, a known card sharp who put a bullet in his own head or was murdered by the San Francisco police in 1905; James De Witt Andrews, a Northwestern University law professor; W. E. Sanders, a Colorado mining magnate; and a pair of E. S. Andrews (our nom de plume backward), one an agent for the Chicago & Northwestern Railroad, the other, a Midwestern con man.

view. More than a century after its publication, *The Expert* remains a key source on technical sleight of hand with cards.

Cheating Today

It's no news that poker is hugely popular. But how safe is it? The short answer: It depends on where you play. Casino poker rooms are generally safe. You may be wiped out by superior play, but gone are the days when the mob controlled the industry and cheating was rampant. Today, every aspect of the game is monitored and regulated; dealers must shuffle, cut, and deal in highly prescribed ways to prevent sleight-of-hand manipulation; automatic shuffling machines rule out scams like stacking, location play, and holding out; and everyone—players and employees—remains under constant surveillance from the unblinking eye in the sky. Moreover, the casinos are continuously scrutinized by state gaming boards. To the extent that cheating does occur in casino poker rooms, it is in the form of collusion among certain players against other players, or against the house. Casinos have no need to cheat customers to get their money, and every reason to protect them. The safer the environment, the greater the profits.

Private games, however, are as vulnerable as they ever were, and most of the venerable cheating systems of past centuries are still in use today, albeit with further refinements and new applications. Who's looking out for your interests when you play at the firehouse fund-raiser, social club, fraternal organizations, or underground "poker club"? Or at the weekly game with friends, office buddies, and the occasional "friend of a friend," who drops in, wipes everyone out, and is never seen again? Whether anyone's cheating in your game I couldn't possibly know (although, if you regularly play for high stakes, I'd vote yes). But I'd wager that every scam explained in this book—even the most ancient—is in use today by someone, somewhere. Games go in and out of fashion, but human nature has remained the same, and so have the tricks of the trade, whether the game is stud, draw, baseball, or Texas hold 'em, which, by the way, is vulnerable to at least a half dozen of the scams in this book.

A Note to the Reader

Throughout the book the cheat is referred to in the masculine. This is for convenience only. Many of the best professional cheats are women.

Technical descriptions assume that the reader is right-handed and that the deck is held in the left hand when the cards are dealt. In most instances, the left-handed reader can substitute left for right and the results will be the same. I have also assumed that the reader knows the rules of the most popular poker games.

1

BEATING THE CUT— THREE BOLD MANEUVERS

Trust everyone but always cut the cards.
—Old cowboy saying

Cheating in social or "soft" games is nearly always done by the dealer, working solo or in collusion with a partner. In most at-home games, the deal moves around the table in a clockwise direction. The player whose turn it is to deal gathers the cards from the previous round, shuffles the deck, announces the game, and deals. Before he distributes the cards, however, the dealer must place the pack in front of the player to his right so that it may be cut. One function of the cut is to begin the deal at a random spot. More important, however, if the dealer is a cheat and has secretly positioned any known cards on the top or bottom of the pack, a cut buries those cards and foils the deception. Overcoming the cut, therefore, is one of the chief problems the cheat must cope with. S. W. Erdnase—the first great cheat to publish his methods— called the cut the "bête noire" of the cheater's existence. How do you get around it?

Amazingly, the cheat has many options. So many, in fact, that to avoid overload I have spread the information over several entries. To begin, here are three bold approaches.

1. The Psych-Out   The cheat's goal here is to brainwash his opponent so that he decides *not* to cut the cards. The cheat does this by appearing to cut the cards himself—selling the idea that no additional cut is necessary. Actually, the cut is false. Upon squaring the pack in the hands, the cheat uses his right forefinger at the front end of the pack to swivel the top half of the deck to the left, where it is taken by the left hand (Fig. 1). The right hand tables its cards, comes back for the rest of the deck, and places them on top of the tabled portion. It looks like a cut but isn't. For the psych-out to work, the cheat performs the false cut with authority, vigorously slapping

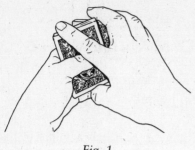

Fig. 1

the cards to the table in what appears to be a macho, manly cut. The fish may now take the bait or not.

2. Bullying A more brazen strategy is to run roughshod over the company and not offer the pack for cutting. The slithery bottom-dealer Worm (Ed Norton) in the movie *Rounders* does this all the time. He shuffles and deals and no one calls him on it (although he is eventually pummeled to a pulp when caught *in flagrante delicto* dealing from the cellar). Not offering the deck for cutting goes against all convention but it happens in soft games when nobody speaks up. When a player does object, the cheat apologizes for his oversight and the next time chooses a more subtle weapon, such as "the jump."

3. The Jump The brilliant French conjuror Robert-Houdin explained this technique, drawn from the Parisian underworld, in his *Card Sharpers—Their Tricks Exposed or the Art of Always Winning* (1861). The deck is placed on the table for cutting. The designated cutter lifts off a packet of cards and places them to the left of the bottom packet. This is standard procedure; normally the dealer completes the cut by placing the bottom portion of the deck on top of the cut-off portion. Instead, the cheat picks up the bottom half of the deck with his right hand and immediately transfers it to his left. He then picks up the remainder of the deck—the original top section—and adds it to the left-hand cards. For some reason this not only looks honest, it can *feel* honest. In a variation, the right hand *slides* the original bottom half to the edge of the table where it is taken by the waiting left hand. The right hand goes back for the remaining cards and slides them off the table to join the rest.

Can cheats actually get away with these kinds of tricks and ploys? Not in fast company. But in a casual game, performed with the requisite nonchalance, absolutely. For one thing, the moves are not as obvious as they seem. Second, most people in a soft game don't pay attention. And most important, the skilled manipulator, whether card sharp or conjuror, conceals his technique beneath a blanket of ordinary appearances which render the moves invisible. In magical parlance, cloaking technique is known as "misdirection"; in the universe of crooked gambling, the word is "shade." A simple but effective diversion is to ask a question while doing the work. "Is the pot light?" "Anyone object to a game of Chicago?" A question requires a response. The players look at the pot, at each other—and the move breezes by.

Prevention and Detection

No matter how honest you believe the dealer to be, never decline the cut. When another player waves it off, he is either an accomplice or naïve. Call for the cut yourself. Don't let a player shuffle and deal. Speak up. No offense, friend, but where I come from we always cut the cards. Watch for trickery as the dealer *completes* the cut. *Lots of shenanigans happen at exactly this point.* The jump is only the beginning. Did I say cut the cards?

2

COLLUSION—WORKING THE TELEGRAPH

The first and original ground of Cheating is a counterfeit countenance in all things; A study to seem to be and not to be in deed.
—Gilbert Walker (1552)

Collusion or team cheating is easily the chief threat to the average player. In its most basic form, secret communication through a set of prearranged signals, it requires no technical skill with cards, is virtually undetectable, impossible to prove, and can be utilized every hand since it doesn't matter who deals. In the parlance of old-time card hustlers, exchanging information was known as "working the telegraph," or "giving office," an "office" being any kind of signal. This type of collusion is common wherever poker is played.

The work: The cheats agree on a secret language—it can be spoken or silent—and use it to reveal hand strength, conspire on betting strategies, and analyze opponents' hands. The conversation is conducted openly but invisibly. Charlie places a chip on his hole card. George adjusts his glasses. Translation: *Jack-high flush. Beats my hand, go for it.* If cheats did nothing but exchange this kind of information, they would come out ahead. Here are the three most common applications.

Playing Best Hand Every time the cards are dealt, the cheats "discuss" which of them holds the superior hand, and the other player drops out. In the short run the team may win or lose that particular hand, but in the long run they always come out ahead. As Darwin Ortiz points out in his classic *Gambling Scams* (1984), playing best hand is tantamount to being dealt two poker hands while everyone else receives only one, and then having the option of which hand to play. Obviously, the superior hand has the better chance of winning the pot, but perhaps not so obvious is the possibility that the weaker hand is a strong, playable hand that would normally remain in the game until the end—only to lose. By *not* playing the hand, the cheats end up with more money in their collective pocket at the end of the night.

Put another way, playing best hand doubles the chances of winning and reduces the losses by half. Every time an honest player *wins* the pot, he's being cheated. As simple as the scam seems, it is very powerful.

A relative of best hand is "playing cousins." A group of cronies who hang out in the same casino or public card room tacitly agree not to compete with each other, but to target the steady stream of tourists and clueless amateurs who make the mistake of sitting at their table. These players have no financial stake in each other. They don't split profits at the end. What they do is get out of each other's way, agree not to bluff each other, and let the one with the best hand go head to head with the mark. The strategy can be as simple as one player signaling his cohorts, "I've got a pair of aces—if you can't beat me, fold." Again, the honest player is cheated because the pots are never what they would be if every man played for himself.

Crossfire   The cheats trap their victims in a crossfire of raises and reraises intended to squeeze every possible cent from the player sandwiched in the middle. This kind of pot building works in any game, but is especially common in hi-lo where players on the draw often stick around for several rounds to see how the hands shape up. Player A, with a lock on low, bets and signals his partner, player D, to raise. Meanwhile, B and C call the bet. D has a weak hand and should fold, but raises instead. Player A reraises, and players B and C are trapped in the middle. Even if an honest player ends up splitting the pot, if more than two players were caught in the crossfire, the cheats come out ahead. This technique is also known as "whipsaw" and "middling."

Conversely, a fusillade of hefty raises can be used to drive the competition *out* of the game. Three quick raises in the early rounds is often all it takes for the cheats to steal the blinds or antes. This ploy is often used when the cheats hold marginal hands. In late rounds, the scam is more transparent but nonetheless effective in driving out any players still on the draw. It is to prevent this type of collusion that card rooms have a maximum number of raises—but the strategy still works. The fewer players in the game, the more effective the scheme.

Signaling for Dead Cards   Players skilled at signaling can also exchange information so as to more accurately read their opponent's hands. Consider a hold 'em scenario in which four spades are on the board and the cheat has the king of spades in the hole. The only card he's afraid of is the ace. So he taps his index finger once on the end of his pocket cards and his partner leans forward in his chair. Translation: *Did anyone hold the ace of spades? Yes!* The cheat now knows he's home free.

While this may seem like a rare occurrence, comparable situations arise all the time. An opponent has a pair of aces on the board and a third ace is elsewhere on the table. Does the player have trips (three of a kind)? Not if one of the cheats can account for the fourth ace. Exchanging this type of information is known as *signaling for dead cards* and can be very valuable anytime the cheat fears a single card.

Prevention and Detection

Collusion is tough to beat. Playing best hand is virtually undetectable. The cheat who folds with a strong hand makes sure to bury his cards in the muck, leaving no evidence. And while it's not difficult to recognize that you're caught in a crossfire, proving collusion is almost impossible. There are, however, precautions to take and telltale signs to watch for.

First, at the risk of stating the obvious, never sit down at a card room or casino table where you've observed the same cast of characters always playing together. Second, during the course of a game be on the lookout for *patterns of illogical betting.* When a player habitually *raises* and then *folds,* an alarm should sound. What gives? Was he bluffing? Was he pumping up the pot for a partner, or trying to steam-roll the competition? Was he a total idiot at cards? We can't be certain because we never see his hand. And that, precisely, is what should trigger the alarm. Lots of betting and we never see the cards. Likewise, be wary of the player who habitually bets a bundle and when called has nothing to show for it. The same questions apply. The red flag is not a single instance of illogical play, but a pattern. The less sense the betting makes in retrospect, the more likely you're being screwed. Do the math and get out of the game.

EARLY WARNINGS

The earliest mention of collusion at the card table is found in *Of the Subtleties, Ruses, Deceits, Cheating and Nasty Things That Are Done in Games* by the Parisian expert Olivier Gouyn (1550). English authors issued warnings soon after: Gilbert Walker in *A Manifest Detection of the Most Vile and Detestable Use of Diceplay, and Other Practices Like the Same* (1552) and Robert Greene in *A Notable Discovery of Cozenage* (1591).

Last, you might heed the advice your mother gave you and never play cards with strangers. But even that is no guarantee of an honest game.

MORE COLLUSIVE TACTICS

Colluders will often bump heads and put on a show for the other players. In a heads-up situation, the cheats may play aggressively and with feigned hostility, or they may adapt a loosey-goosey style to coax the competition into more freewheeling play. At the end of the night, if one of the cheats is sitting on buckets of ill-gotten cash, he may disarm the competition by losing everything to one or more of his partners in a sudden streak of rotten luck. In tournament play, one cheat may deliberately lose to his partner in order to feed him chips and propel him into the next round well armed.

3

TABLE TALK—HOW COLLUDERS COMMUNICATE

Most cheats are clever enough to invent their own signaling systems. But for those who prefer the tried and true, the literature of cheating is chock-full of methods, from "working the telegraph"—tugging on a wire strung under the table between the cheats—to miniature transmitters and receivers that deliver messages via tiny shocks or vibrations. Most of the serious cheats, however, avoid anything that could turn into physical evidence; they rely on verbal codes or embed their messages in gestures and body language. Many ingenious systems are possible. Consider the following:

Verbal Codes   Anything that can pass for normal poker-table conversation can be used to code information. Phrases like "check," "I check," "I'm going to check," can be signals to a partner to bet, fold, or raise. Specific cards are indicated by specific words. In one system currently in use the word "time" indicates a ten. So when the cheat says "What's the time?" he may be signaling for dead cards (Anyone have a ten?) or revealing that he's got one. Obviously, any word can be tied to any card, and with 52 easy-to-use key words, it's a snap to ask for or reveal any card. Many a vaudeville mind-reading act worked along the same principles.

Hand Signals   The same type of information can be revealed nonverbally. A hand resting on the table with one, two, or three fingers extended can indicate the cheat holds a pair, two pair, or trips. In draw poker, hand strength can be conveyed by fanning the cards so that one card is slightly higher than the others, indicating a pair, two pair, trips, straight, or flush. An open hand resting on the table is universally recognized as cheaters' code for "all is well," while a closed fist signals "heat," or danger, and calls off the play in progress.

To code specific cards, cheats use a century-old system based on finger position. The index finger stretched across the short end of the card indicates an ace; two fingers means a king; a finger on the corner signifies a queen, and so forth. A similar code combines finger position with how deeply the cards are held in the hand. An index finger on the end of the card indicates an ace; a quarter of the way down, a king; halfway down, a queen, and so forth. Like spoken codes, hand signals are used to ask for and indicate "dead cards," and to let a crooked dealer know what card the signaler would like to have, should the dealer get his hands on it.

Positioning Codes   In five-card stud, a classic method of revealing the value of the hole card is based on the position of the up-card relative to the pocket card. If the cards are square, the hole card is an ace; if the up-card is angled slightly to the right, a king is indicated; angled a bit more equals a queen, and so forth.

In a hold 'em scenario, the pocket cards can be indicated by the simple expedient of pinning the cards with a few chips. Both suit and value can be revealed by *where* the chips are placed on the card (center, off-center, which corner, or any combination thereof), *how many* chips are placed, and the *value* of the chips. Cheating teams will code this information as a matter of course, since any information can become valuable at any time.

Mucking Codes   In this ingenious system, *how* the cheat mucks (discards) his cards indicates what they are. Are they *pushed* toward the dealer, *spun* across the table, sent *together* or *singly*? Are the cards mucked immediately when it's the player's turn to act, or is there a delay of a second or two? Each of these actions can have an agreed-on meaning, and can be extremely useful in the early rounds of hold 'em. For example, if a cheat sees that his partner has just mucked a ten, pre-flop, he may think twice about the value of his pocket tens.

The Glance This final example comes from Robert-Houdin's *Card Sharpers—Their Tricks Exposed or the Art of Always Winning*. The code is based entirely on "glances" and the position of the mouth. To indicate a king, the cheat simply looks at his partner; to indicate a queen, he looks at an opponent; a glance at the pot signifies a jack, while looking across the room indicates an ace. Suits are coded by the position of the mouth: open, closed, upper lip on lower or lower lip on upper, indicating hearts, diamonds, clubs, or spades. To signal that he holds the jack, queen, and ace of hearts, the cheat "directs successively his looks on the play of the opponent, on the stakes, and on the opposite side, always keeping the mouth slightly open."

These systems represent the tip of the iceberg. Every card in the deck can be coded by how the cheat smokes a cigarette (how many fingers hold the cigarette, which hand it's in, and in what part of the mouth), or by how an object, such as a cigarette lighter, is placed on the table within an imaginary grid. Actually, there's no keeping up with the methods. What matters in the end are not the specifics of a code, but the recognition that signaling plays a central role in many scams. To summarize: The cheat will use signals (1) to indicate hand strength in the context of "best hand" or "cousins"; (2) to initiate a crossfire; (3) to ask for or reveal "dead cards"; (4) to request a specific card to complete a hand; and (5) to disclose hole cards and discards, enabling accomplices to play with the maximum amount of information.

Prevention and Detection

Unless the cheats are rank amateurs, all of these systems will slip under the radar. So how can you tell if you're surrounded by invisible chatter? You can't. But if you find hand after hand playing out as if you were surrounded by mind readers, you may want to cut your losses and call it a night.

THE DA VINCI CODE

Leonardo da Vinci is known to have been fascinated by codes, mirror writing, and cryptography. So it's not surprising that he is also credited with the first published method for secretly coding the identity of a playing card to an accomplice. The method—which is given in the context of a magic trick—appears in *De viribus quantitatis* (On the Powers of Numbers, circa 1550) by da Vinci and the Franciscan monk Luca Pacioli. The performer has a card selected and it is mysteriously named by a young boy across the room. The modus operandi involves a simple set of prearranged hand signals that the magician (who knows the card) secretly flashes to his assistant. Conjuring scholar William Kalush considers *De viribus* to be the first book devoted primarily to magic tricks, most of them mathematical.

4

THE LAY STACK

This cunning technique gives the poker cheat virtual X-ray vision. Without the use of marked cards or sleight of hand, he immediately knows every hole card on the table.

The secret of the trick is memory. The cheat begins by memorizing a sequence of cards during the hand prior to his deal. To use a simple example, we'll ignore the suits and say the cards are A-6-K-4-4 and they comprise the cheat's hand in a game of draw poker. Rather than play the hand, the cheat drops out and puts the cards facedown on the table, remembering their order. When all the cards are tossed over for the next deal, the cheat positions the five memorized cards on top of the deck. A false shuffle and bogus cut later, and the cheat calls five-card stud—the perfect game to exploit this situation—and deals. In a five-handed game, every down-card is now known to the cheat in clockwise order, A-6-K-4-4.

In the taxonomy of cheating, this is a form of "stacking the deck." Unlike most stacks, however, the cards are not arranged in a predetermined order nor are they intended to produce a winning hand—only an enormous advantage. Because the cards are utilized in the order in which they are found, or "as they lay," the technique is known as "lay stacking," and the memorized cards are "a lay stack."

Obviously, the more cards the cheat can memorize, the greater his advantage (an advantage that is doubled when the cheat is able to convey the identity of these cards to a confederate through signaling). Ten memorized cards and the cheat knows *both* pocket cards in five-player hold 'em or seven-card stud. To memorize a longer sequence, the cheat again remembers his own hand and drops out. When the next player folds, his cards are added to the cheat's, but not before the hustler looks at and memorizes a few. This is done casually and openly, and the cheat makes no attempt to rearrange the cards. They are simply glanced at, memorized, and set aside, eventually winding up on top of the pack.

Despite its simplicity, or perhaps because of it, this cheating strategy is extraordinarily efficient, producing large payoffs for little work. True, there is no predicting which player will win any particular hand. But equally true, the cheat and his partners have a gargantuan advantage. They know when to raise, when to fold, who is bluffing, and who has the best hand. These are the strongest advantages a player can have. Given the choice of holding high cards, or reading his opponent like an open book, the cheat will always go for the later.

Finally, it should also be noted that this use of a lay stack is exactly the kind of cheating that can in go on in an underground card club or local hold 'em tournament. All that's required is a corrupt house dealer and one or more associates. In this case, the dealer memorizes one or more of the face-up sequences in front of him, rather than the discards. This is relatively easy to do, as the dealer is *supposed* to study the exposed cards to verify the winner. In studying them, he memorizes a string and later maneuvers them to the top of the deck. He then quarterbacks the next hand by signaling all the pertinent information to his allies. The signals are minimal: check, bet, raise, fold. It is highly doubtful whether anyone will recognize the cards of a previous hand turning up, successively, during the next deal.

Detection and Prevention

Because the use of a lay stack involves no overt manipulation or rearrangement of the cards, it is extremely difficult to detect. Indeed, even if you suspect what's going on, there's no evidence to uncover, no card up the sleeve, no slug of high cards on the bottom of the deck, no prearranged winner. Attention, therefore, must be focused on the procedures leading up to the deal, as the deal itself is legitimate. Are discrete packets of discards being kept off to the side? Do these end up on top of the pack, or the bottom? Watch for the basics discussed elsewhere: crimps, bridges, false shuffles, and bogus cuts.

THE ART OF MEMORY

Most top card players have steel-trap card memories. Poker pros can name every up-card that's been folded. Bridge experts recall every trick that's been played. How do they do it? Practice, practice, practice. Plus, it doesn't hurt to have a system.

Memory training dates back to the ancient world, where prior to the discovery of hold 'em, Greek and Roman orators used mnemonic tricks to recall long speeches with unfailing accuracy. The key to most systems is creating a series of striking images that will stick in the mind and come to the fore when needed.

In his instructive *Perfecting Your Card Memory*, Charles Edwards suggests learning by rote a set of 52 "characters" each corresponding to a card in the deck. For ease of recall, all of the club-suit characters begin with the letter C (Ace = *Cockroach*, 2 = *Cat*, 3 = *Car*), the diamonds with D (Ace = *Doctor*, 2 = *Detective*), and so forth. To memorize a sequence such as A/C, 2/C, 3/C, 2/D, the character images are brought to mind and pasted together to form a story line, the more bizarre the better. You might, for example, visualize a gigantic *cockroach* wrapping its hairy legs around Garfield the *cat* who leaps into the air and crashes down through the roof of a *car* driven by the *detective* Sherlock Holmes. To recall the sequence, all you need do is remember the *cockroach*, and the *cat*, *car*, and *detective* should spring to mind. The more exaggerated, raunchy, comic, or gross the images are, the easier they are to remember. For other approaches check out *Learn to Remember* (Chronicle Books, 2000) by Dominic O'Brien, and Harry Lorayne's classic *The Memory Book* (Ballantine Books, reissued 1996).

5

FORCING THE CUT—
THE BRIDGE

Here is another approach to nullifying the cut. Imagine the hustler has three kings on the bottom of the deck that he intends to deal to a partner. If the pack is legitimately cut, the kings end up in the center of the deck and the plan is ruined. The solution? Begin with monarchs in the middle—and have the mark cut them back to the bottom! This strategy, known as "forcing the cut," is engineered with a piece of mini architecture known as a "bridge," or "saddle." Basically, it is a bend in one or more cards which is used to mark and then "force" the location of the cut.

As is often the case, the dirty work is done during a sequence of continuous operations. We pick up the action here after the cheat has false-shuffled, retaining the kings on the bottom, and squared the pack. The right hand now cuts about half the cards to the table, beginning a legitimate cut. At the same time, the left hand secretly puts a convex bend along the length of the remaining cards by squeezing them between the fingers and the heel of the hand. The index finger, curled under the deck, pushes upward to start the bridge in the proper direction (Fig. 1). This is done in a split second—just squeeze and release. The right hand now returns for the rest of the pack and places it neatly on the tabled half. The pack is now picked up, squared in the hands, and set back on the table, inviting the cut (Fig. 2). If the mark cuts any-where *near* the bridge he will very likely cut *at* the bridge,

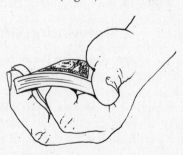

Fig. 1

Fig. 2

as the flesh of the thumb and fingers automatically enter the notched portion of the pack. The cheat then completes the cut, restoring the deck to its original order. In a variation, the cheat can also "put in the work" during an in-the-hands cut. As the right hand transfers a packet from the top of the deck to the bottom, the left hand puts in the bend. Once the pack is back in the original order, a final bend of the entire deck will restore a uniform appearance.

While not infallible, forcing the cut usually works. Moreover, the cheat can increase his chances of success by observing where his opponent typically cuts the pack. Many players habitually cut at the same spot—near the top, bottom, or center. Observing this, the dealer adjusts his procedure so as to situate the bridge in the desired location. Indeed, according to Erdnase, who never overlooked a technical refinement, the canny cheat takes care to set the pack down at precisely the right angle to the cutter "so that the hand which the player habitually uses will come naturally into the most favorable position to oblige the dealer." When the player seated at the dealer's right is an accomplice, cutting to the right spot is guaranteed.

Prevention and Detection

The larger the bridge the more likely someone will cut to it. By the same token, the wider the gap the easier it is to detect. If you suspect foul play, look for bridgework. Observe the dealer. Is he bending or unbending portions of the pack? Are the cards warped, bent, or otherwise deformed? If so, point it out and ask for a fresh deck. Vary the depth at which you cut. The more unpredictable you are, the tougher to exploit.

BUILDING OTHER BRIDGES

The basic bridge is most effective when the deck is cut by the ends. Should the sharper need to build a bridge along the length of the deck—to accommodate those who cut the pack by the sides—he begins by giving the deck a riffle shuffle followed by a "waterfall flourish" (Fig. 3). This puts a *convex* bend in the entire pack. As the cards are squared, the right thumb and fingers grasp the top half of the pack by the ends and pull upward, giving these cards a *concave* bend (the left thumb lies across the width of the pack and maintains a downward pressure). The deck is then cut in the hands and the bridge is in place.

Fig. 3

6

CULLING

You can observe a lot by watching.
—Yogi Berra

Before the cheat can deal himself the fabled four aces, he must first locate and position the aces. Before he can produce a royal straight flush in spades, he needs to marshal the troops; the 10, J, Q, K, A of spades. This phase of the cheating operation—locating and isolating cards to be used in the upcoming deal—is known as culling. It's the hunting-gathering stage of crooked dealing.

To be sure, the cheat rarely culls a royal straight flush; it's way too obvious and the stuff of poker movies. Instead, he seeks out strong pairs, threes of a kind, even straights and flushes, finding them among the discards, or lying openly on the table. The cards are assembled on the offbeat; between hands or during actions peripheral to the game. Then, when the moment is right, the targeted cards are brought to the top or bottom of the deck where they are dealt, stacked or repositioned according to plan. Here's how.

The Discard Cull   In this cull, the cheat recruits candidates for an upcoming hand by browsing through the discards. This is against all the rules of sane poker playing but, amazingly, it's tolerated in many social games where it is perceived as idle curiosity. The cheat gets himself into this position by dropping out on the hand prior to his deal, so that all the deadwood is tossed his way. A quick look through the muck (discards) is usually all it takes to find some ammo. The target cards aren't pulled from the discards and openly rearranged. Instead, as the cheat thumbs the cards from hand to hand, the right fingers slide the desired cards *under* the spread, which is angled to avoid detection, and the target cards are gathered at the bottom of the packet. One ace joins another. A pair becomes trips. Often, a high pair can be found together and cut to the top or bottom of the packet to start the cull. As soon as the cheat has what he wants, he sets the discards set aside and ignores them. When the remaining cards are tossed over for the new deal, the cheat drops the incoming cards directly on top of his culled cards (if he wants them on the bottom of the deck), or adds the culled cards to the top of the heap. The cheat can also cull from the talon (the undealt cards) after all the hands have been dealt. The usual ploy to justify looking through the stub is "to see if I would have made my hand." In reality, it's the next hand the cheat is concerned with.

Cards can also be culled in the act of squaring the deck. As the cards are tossed his way for the new deal, the cheat rakes them in, turns the faceup cards facedown, and pushes them all together in an uneven pile. The cards are then turned to a vertical position, faces inward, and squared by tapping and rotating all the jutting cards so they can be pushed flush. Under cover of these actions, however, the cheat uses his thumbs to actually splay the cards further so that he can spot target cards and shift them to the top or bottom of the pack (Fig. 1). The straightening of the cards provides a deceptive cover under which cards can be strategically stripped out and shuttled into position with very little motion.

With two cheats conspiring, a powerful hand can be culled in very short order. The cheat's ally signals that he's got, say, four hearts that will be coming over for the next deal; moreover, the hearts will be on top of the discarded hand. Now all the dealer has to do is cull one more heart and he's ready to stack a flush for himself or his partner.

Fig. 1

The Pickup Cull   Here culling is done in the act of clearing the table after the showdown. This is more deceptive than discard culling since there are no obvious tells, such as looking through the discards. The cheat prepares for the moment by surveying the up-cards on the board, looking for winning combinations. In a stud game, seven players, there can be as many as 28 up-cards to choose from (unlikely, but possible). The cheat might focus on a pair of aces in one hand, and a single ace from another hand. Or, in a less obvious example, he might see a straight, made by combining a 7-9-J from one hand with an 8-10 from another. It's an easy matter, in scooping up the cards, to combine the target cards in any order and bring them to the top or bottom for further manipulation. If the cheat is a bottom dealer, the culled cards go to the bottom of the deck and he's set to go.

In a hold 'em or Omaha scenario, the cheat has less of a selection to cull from. Nonetheless, even a single ace delivered to the cheat's hand will tilt the odds in his favor. Or, better still, the cheat can memorize and cull *all* of the community cards to the top of the deck, and, following a false shuffle and cut, deal them as is. This is another form of the lay stack, but done more openly. The cheat automatically knows the first five hole cards, or even the first eight, if he can glimpse the burn cards and add them to the cull.

Prevention and Detection

Discard culling can be done rapidly and invisibly. What can't be rendered invisible is the act of *looking* through the discards. It's called rabbit hunting, and it's open season for cheating. Prevent that and you prevent at least one form of discard culling. Shouting "Hey, no looking through the discards" will usually do the trick.

Pickup culls go undetected primarily because they take place "out of frame." A game unit starts with a series of shuffles; then cards are dealt, betting occurs, a winner is declared, and the game is over. The next game unit doesn't begin, and attention doesn't refocus, until the new dealer starts to shuffle. What happens in between—the tossing-in of hands, assembling cards, passing them to the new dealer—is given scant attention. The cheat does the dirty work out in the open, but because it's out of frame, it's easy to miss.

Culling is the essential first step to bottom dealing, stacking, and many location plays. Make it a point to follow how the cards are picked up. Is it really haphazard, or is there a method to the madness? And remember, no looking through the discards!

7

FALSE RIFFLE SHUFFLES

*One of the most important differences between man
and other species is the opposable thumb, which
allows man to both overhand and riffle shuffle.*
—Steve Beam

Crooked dealers have at their fingertips an amazing repertoire of false shuffles, each with its own purpose and place at the card table. For everyday scamming, the most useful of these are the *partial* false shuffles. These enable the cheat to openly and honestly shuffle *most* of the cards while preserving a select group of cards on the top or bottom of the deck for later use. The mechanics are surprisingly simple, but there's no need for overkill. As we'll later see, the cheat will add finishing touches like counterfeit "boxing" and "stripping" that give the entire sequence the look and feel of a genuine casino shuffle.

False In-the-Hands Riffle Shuffle   This shuffle resembles what goes on in most home games. The deck is held vertically in the right hand and the right thumb riffles off about half the pack into the waiting left fingers (Fig. 1). The left hand takes control of its cards, mirroring the right, and the two packets are riffled together so that the cards interlace. This is an honest shuffle.

Deception enters the picture as the cheat keeps the top or bottom slug *out of* the shuffling process. As most card players discover on their own, this is easily done by controlling the speed of the riffles, and which packets begin and end the shuffles.

Fig. 1

This is the principle behind all of the false shuffles described here. To preserve the bottom stock, the deck is split as described and the left hand begins the shuffle. As soon as the slug is riffled off, the right hand joins the action and the rest of the shuffle is genuine. This is very simple, but it works.

Controlling top stock is a bit trickier, as the cheat can't take the direct course and end each shuffle with the top stock. The ruse would be too obvious. So the cheat adds a throw-off: He holds back one or two cards from the left hand and *adds* them to the top of the deck at the end of each shuffle. Then he switches to an overhand shuffle (see the 27th Way, "The Jog Shuffle") and *removes* the added cards by running them singly into the left hand and throwing the rest of the deck on top. Alternating between overhand and riffle shuffles is common in home games and won't raise an eyebrow.

The cheat will also enhance the deceptiveness of the shuffle by squaring the pack on its long sides after each shuffle, deliberately exposing the bottom cards to interested parties. The cheat makes sure to begin each shuffle with the right hand's packet, ensuring that the bottom card continually changes. Although a very sloppy way to shuffle, it takes the heat off the top of the deck and sells the illusion that all the cards are being mixed.

False Table Riffle Shuffle   This shuffle mimics the regulation shuffle used in casinos and serious-money games. The cards are kept flat on the table to prevent flashing; no waterfall flourishes, no squaring the pack on its sides. If you're up against a crooked house dealer, this is the shuffle he'll use.

To maintain the bottom stock, the right hand cuts the top *third* of the deck to the right and both hands angle their packets into a shallow V-shape formation. The fingers cover the outer edges of the cards, and the thumbs lift the inner corners of the packets (Fig. 2). As soon as the left hand has riffled off the bot-

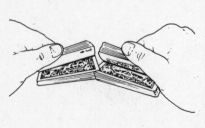

Fig. 2

tom stock, the right hand joins in and both hands deplete their packets simultaneously. Because the left hand's packet is larger, the shuffle can start and end with the left hand. This makes it very clear that the top cards change positions after every shuffle. The shuffle is known as a *lopsided riffle shuffle*.

Controlling top stock deceptively again requires a bit of finesse, as the top of the deck is more open to observation. In one sequence designed to fool the eye, the cheat cuts half the deck to the *right* for one shuffle and to the *left* for the next, always ending the riffles with the original top stock. The top card remains in view, but the shuttling action, simple as it is, makes it very difficult to follow what's happening, especially when three or four shuffles are done rapidly in succession.

Eventually, however, the cheat will take the top card out of sight. This is done by adding a single card from the left packet and then subtracting it with a maneuver known as a slip cut. Here's a typical sequence. The right hand cuts the top of the deck to the right and the packets are interlaced, ending with the top stock. The shuffle is repeated, only this time the left thumb holds back a single card and drops it on top, burying the original top card. The deck is now squared and gripped by the corners, between the thumbs and middle fingers. The right hand pulls the top half of the deck to the right, *except* for the top card, which is held back by the left index finger (Fig. 3). The right hand's cards are raised and slapped back onto the rest of the deck. The illusion of a genuine cut is excellent, as the top card is clearly seen going into the *middle* of the deck. In fact, it is the only card that is displaced, and the setup is back on top.

False riffle shuffles have endless variations. However, all that matters from the cheat's perspective is that the shuffles do what false shuffles are supposed to do: visually appear to mix the cards, emotionally reassure the players that the game is honest, and

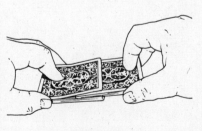

Fig. 3

clandestinely maintain known cards in a known position. What's next depends on the cheat's plan.

Detection and Prevention

It is easy to be beguiled by the cheat's manner as he appears to pay no attention to the cards as he shuffles, carries on a conversation, and mulls over what game he might call next. Knowing about false shuffles, how they work and how good they can look, is half the battle. Whenever possible, keep your eyes on the top and bottom cards. Do they change places after every shuffle? If your view of the cards is obscured by a tight shuffle, request that the shuffle be conducted more openly.

Be certain that any shuffling sequence is followed by a genuine cut. If you don't trust what's going on, cut the cards yourself. Better yet, remember that *every player has the right to shuffle the cards before the deal*. The dealer is entitled to the final shuffle, but one thorough shuffle on your part will undo any serious mischief.

8

THE TOP CARD PEEK

Teacher: *I hope I just didn't see you cheating, Billy.*
Billy: *Me too!*

One of the strongest advantages a player can have is knowing the top card of the deck before it's dealt. Marked cards do the trick but are inherently risky and subject to discovery. Sophisticated cheats prefer an anytime, anywhere approach. They peek. Here are three methods of secretly glimpsing the top card, along with several canny applications.

The Riffle Peek This easy and effective peek occurs as the cheat riffle shuffles the deck prior to dealing. The deck is divided into two approximately equal packets, and the inner corners are interlaced as they riffle off the thumbs. On the last shuffle, the cheat controls the riffle so that the final card falls from the left packet. Just before the card is released, the cheat glances down, and the index is clearly visible (Fig. 1).

This peek is extremely powerful in home games when the cheat has an ally seated to his left. If the peeked card is a deuce, for example, the dealer calls a game with deuces wild; if it's a three or a nine, he calls Baseball; for the ace of spades, it's Chicago.

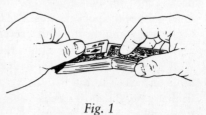

Fig. 1

What starts out seeming like a small advantage—glimpsing a single card—can often be parlayed into a sure thing.

The resourceful cheat can further exploit the riffle peek by trawling for valuable cards as he shuffles. He simply ends each shuffle with a peek. If a desirable card appears, he stops shuffling and moves on to the false cut. If not, he cuts the top half of the pack to the right and peeks at a fresh card from the left packet. This is very sneaky.

The Bubble Peek   This peek can occur anytime during play. It is the preferred method for stud games, where the deck often remains in the dealer's hands throughout the game. If you don't know what to look for, you won't see it.

The deck is held in a left-hand dealing grip, the outer right corner cradled between the index and middle finger, the ring and pinkie fingers along the side, and the thumb at the outer left corner. To peek at the top card, two things happen at once. The left

Fig. 2

hand rotates at the wrist, turning back up, and the left thumb firmly pushes the top card to the right. Because the card has no place to go—the left fingers acting as a stop—the upper right corner of the card "bubbles up," exposing the index to the cheat's downward glance (Fig. 2). With a little extra pressure, two cards can be exposed at the same time.

A common cover for making the peek is checking hole cards. The cheat uses both hands to lift the inner ends of the pocket cards. The left hand, holding the inverted deck, is apparently there to prevent exposing the cards to the player on the left. At this moment, the card is peeked (Fig. 3).

A peek can also be made with the deck perpendicular to the table and close to the body. In that case, the move needs more cover. Some sharpers keep a drink or a stack of chips to their left for just this purpose. As the right hand moves across the body to pick up the drink, the left hand "gets out of the way" by moving toward the chest,

Fig. 3

and the peek is made by looking straight down. The right forearm briefly screens the deck from view as the peek is made.

The Heel Peek   Instead of peeking at the outer right index of the top card, the inner left index is viewed instead. Figure 4 shows the final position as the card is glimpsed. It takes a bit of a knack to lever the card into position using only one hand. In one method, the top card is edged slightly to the right by the left thumb and immediately pushed back and upward by the pinkie—causing the inner left corner to pop up. Or, the left thumb can push diagonally inward from the upper left corner, causing the lower left corner to pop up. The heel of the hand then enters the gap, holding it open as the peek is made. The glimpse can be made as the left

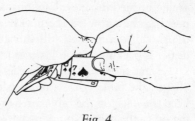

Fig. 4

hand aids in checking hole cards, or pushes chips into the pot. The move is also known as a *back peek*.

If the cheat does nothing more than peek at the top card before dealing, he's way ahead of everyone else. He can foresee that the next player is about to pair up, or make a flush, or not fill a straight, or go bust on a low hand. In Omaha or Texas hold 'em, using a two-card peek, he can signal a partner the identity of the turn and river cards (the fourth and fifth board cards) long before they're turned or rivered. Each play is unique.

Strong as these applications are, a veritable banquet of cheating opportunities is served up when the peek is combined with the second deal, a sleight-of-hand technique that is explored in the 24th Way. Peeking provides knowledge; the second deal puts it to work, big time.

Prevention and Detection

Look out for the player who constantly checks his hole cards with the deck in hand. Every round of dealing provides a fresh card to peek, but the hole cards don't change. So why is the dealer constantly looking at them? Good poker players remember their cards.

Watch out for the telltale wrist turn that accompanies the bubble and heel peeks. This is very easy to miss, as peeking techniques are embedded in natural actions, such as checking hole cards or pushing chips toward the pot. Even if you are aware that these things can occur, they still can go right by. If you suspect the dealer is peeking, watch his eyes as well as his hands.

Casino rules stipulate that the deck must always be held parallel to the table. The same should apply in home games. Also, keep the deck on the table after each round of dealing. No holding on to the deck. No toying with the cards.

9

THE BOTTOM CARD PEEK

Knowing what card lies on the bottom of the deck can be exploited in many sneaky ways. For the bottom dealer the knowledge is essential. But even for the cheat with no sleight-of-hand skills, *any* information not held by the other players is an advantage—even knowing that a particular card will *not* come into play. In hold 'em, for example, it often happens that by the time the game gets to the river, it is clear that only one or two cards can help a particular hand. If the owner of that hand knows that card cannot possibly show up because it's on the bottom of the deck, he drops out and saves money.

Here are two commonly used bottom card peeks. Once the cheat gathers the information he will, of course, share it with his partners.

Rotation Peek   This peek follows a legitimate cut and is accomplished while transferring the deck from one hand to the other. We begin as the cheat tables the deck to his right for the cut. The cutter cuts the top half of the deck to the left, and the cheat completes the cut. He then picks up the deck, thumb on the inner end, fingers on the outer end, and places it into the left hand for dealing. On the way, however, the right hand rotates clockwise at the wrist, bringing the deck to an almost vertical position just before it is taken by the left hand (Fig 1). At that instant,

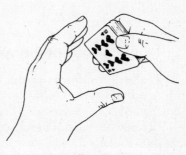

Fig. 1

the cheat glances down and the bottom card is clearly visible. The turning of the deck seems entirely natural and goes right by. The move can be done every time the cheat deals.

Gambler's Bottom-Card Peek   This peek is made in the act of squaring the sides of the pack. It usually follows a shuffle or a cut.

The pack is held in the left hand, the thumb along the left side, the second, ring, and little fingers at the right side, and the index finger lying across the width of the bottom card, at the front end. The right hand holds the pack from above, fingers in front, thumb at the inner end. Now one of two things happens: Either the left hand moves backward and forward, so that the left thumb and fingers can square the sides of the pack, or the left hand remains still and the right hand moves the pack forward and back. In either case, the left index finger maintains upward pressure on the bottom card, causing it to buckle at the inner end, and bringing the index into view (Fig. 2). This is one of those moves that seems

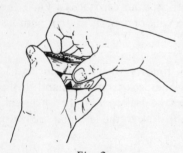

Fig. 2

like it should be obvious to anyone paying attention. In fact, it is invisible from all angles and is over in a trice.

Knowing the bottom card won't affect every hand, but when it does come into play—with the discovery, for example, that an opponent will not be getting that last ace—it's gold.

Prevention and Detection

The back and forth squaring action is the tip-off to the gambler's bottom peek. Usually, it's done briskly and is always accompanied by a downward glance. Watch the dealer's eyes and you'll know for sure. If the cheat is a bottom dealer, you may see this move a lot.

The use of a cut card—an opaque rectangle of plastic the same size as a playing card—will discourage most peekers. After the final shuffle, the card should be placed on the table directly in front of the deck. The cutter lifts a portion of the pack, places it on the cut card and the cut is completed.

It should come as no surprise that tricksters have taken up the challenge of overcoming this precaution. Stay tuned.

10

FLASHING

Flashing is the scammer's version of indecent exposure. The dealer, in the role of exhibitionist, treats his partner to revealing looks at the undersides of cards that, according to the rules, should remain hidden. Flashing techniques are easy to do, hard to spot, and provide an advantage in all forms of poker. This is another example of *multim in parvo*. Put another way: a little goes a long way.

Top Card Flash   This flash gives the cheat's partner a quick look at the card he'll be getting on the next round, enabling him to make an extremely informed decision about how to play his hand. The technique is simple and direct. With the deck in the left hand, the left thumb pushes the top card slightly to the right, and the wrist rotates inward and back, briefly exposing the index of the top card (Fig. 1). In a variation, the top card remains flush with the deck, but the outer right corner is raised by the tip of the left index finger, so that the index is visible as the deck is rotated.

Fig. 1

Getting away with something this bold depends more on timing and misdirection than technical sleight of hand. Usually the cheat will flash on the last card of a dealing round. As the right hand deals the final card, the left wrist rotates back and forth, and then the pack is tabled. Nobody notices because nobody's looking. Each player has a new card to attend to, and the cheat makes sure that his own attention is focused anywhere but on his own left hand. The only one looking there is the cheat's partner, and the move is over in a virtual nanosecond. If the cheat is a second dealer, he can flash the top card to his partner who then signals back whether he wants it or not.

While the flash can be repeated every dealing round (depending on the speed of the company), the cheat usually saves the move for important occasions—especially late in the hand when the cheat's partner may be wondering, "Am I going to make this flush?" Flashing is like the fortune-telling eight ball. Turn it over and the answer appears.

Flashing also has powerful applications to hold 'em and Omaha. In this case, the cheat must get a break under two cards, in order to account for the burn card. The right thumb pushes the cards to the right and immediately pulls them back as the second finger holds open a gap. As in the previous example, a card is flashed at the end of the dealing round; as the cheat deals the last pocket card, he shows his partner the first card of the flop; as he deals the flop he reveals the turn card; and as he deals the turn he flashes the river. Throughout the game, the cheats are a giant step ahead of everybody else. With proper timing and shade, cards can be flashed to any position at the table.

Bottom Card Flash   Rather than revealing what's on the horizon, this flash reveals what won't be coming. The method is the same as the top card flash (a quick wrist turn reveals the index of the bottom card) but the applications, for obvious reasons, are more limited. Most of the time, knowing what's on the bottom will have no relevance to that particular game. In the long run, however, looking pays off, since every ten or fifteen hands, the flashed card will be *exactly* the card the cheat or his opponent needs to win the hand. In the first case the cheat saves money by dropping out, in the second instance he stays in and wins the pot.

Riffle Shuffle Flash   This flash is similar to the top card peek described in the 8th Way. What makes it flashing rather than peeking is that it's the cheat's partner, seated to his right, who glimpses and memorizes the top cards as they riffle off the dealer's left thumb (Fig. 2). The cheat's ally need glimpse only the top

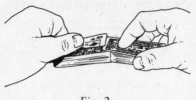

Fig. 2

cards of the final two shuffles to know the identity of the first three or four hole cards. A neutralized cut is necessary to keep the flashed cards in position, but this is no problem. The cheat's partner false-cuts (see "Cutting Class," the 44th Way), cuts at a bridge, or "knuckles the cut," waving it off altogether.

Scramble Flash   In professional card rooms, riffle shuffling is often preceded with a scramble or "wash." The cards are spread facedown over a large area and are mixed together in a circular motion. In the process of consolidating the deck for the upcoming shuffle, the cheat can easily flash several of the bottom cards to his partner as he turns the cards on their long edges and squares the pack. If these cards are retained on the bottom, the cheat's partner has the same advantage as in the bottom card flash, greatly multiplied. The flashed cards can also be cut to the center and used for a location play (see the 21st Way).

Dealing Flash   This maneuver enables the cheat's partner to see the undersides of some of the opponents' cards as they are dealt. It's a crude ploy, but that doesn't stop less sophisticated cheating teams from trying it. The cheat's partner sits as low as possible in his chair, and the dealer sails the cards across the table so that faces are briefly visible from a low angle. While it is difficult to make out the exact identity of the flashed card, it's relatively easy to see whether it's a picture or an ace. Sometimes only one player's cards will be targeted for viewing, which makes the technique a little less obvious. Knowing your opponent has an ace in the hole is not a trivial advantage.

Prevention and Detection

Spotting the wrist turn that accompanies top and bottom card flashing is, theoretically, easy. The hard part is remembering to look for it. Cheats usually play honestly at the start and have a keen sense of when they can start getting away with things. Make it a point, from time to time, to focus on the dealer's hands from start to finish. If you think he's deliberately flashing, watch the eyes of the guy next to him. When you see a dealer turn the deck faceup, point it out. It could be accidental. Then again . . .

Some dealers stand while dealing, especially when having to deal down a long table. Lots of cards get flashed this way, intentionally and accidentally. Instead of sailing the cards, they should be dealt in neat packets in front of the dealer and then slid down to the players. This will prevent even unintentional flashing.

The power of flashing should not be underestimated. Cheats do it all the time.

11

THE PICKUP STACK—
THE DISCARD STACK

*Some men are born rascals, some men have rascality
thrust upon them, others achieve it.*
—George Devol, *Forty Years a Gambler on the Mississippi*

Cheats practiced in the art of the pickup cull (the 6th Way) will often crank up the voltage by culling and stacking at the same time, producing a lethal shocker known as a pickup stack. As the cheat studies the board, he not only zeroes in on the cards he plans to deal to himself in the next game, he also picks out the "x" cards that he will insert *between* the target cards so that they will fall, without further fiddling, to the desired position when the cards are dealt.

Suppose the game is seven-card stud, four players, and the board looks like Fig. 1 just before the showdown.

While there are two straights and a full house among these cards, the cheat will keep things simple and go for the three aces. The goal, remember, is to clear the board and stack the hand at the same time, so that the final arrangement reads, from the top of the deck down, x-x-x-A, x-x-x-A, x-x-x-A, the rest of the deck. But how do you get from here to there?

The cheat has mapped out all his moves like a chess player and starts clearing the board as soon as the winner is declared. The right hand picks up the A-7-10-10 and drops them facedown onto the previous discards so that the ace is on top. The left hand gathers the remaining three cards from the same hand and adds them to the heap (which now reads x-x-x-A). The J-Q are slid under the 9-A, and all four are dropped facedown onto the pile (which now reads from the top down, x-x-x-A, x-x-x-A). Finally, the K-4-4-A, which need no rearranging, are turned facedown as a unit, and dropped on top of everything to complete the stack (x-x-x-A,

Fig. 1

x-x x-A, x-x-x-A). These cards are added to the talon (the undealt cards), or more deceptively, the talon is placed on top of the stack, but the cheat maintains a break between the two sections with his little finger. The deck is then split at the break and false-shuffled so that the stack remains on top. A bogus cut, and the cheat starts his hand with the set.

While all this may sound fussy and a bit daunting, those who do it for a living have no trouble seeing what needs to be done and doing it quickly and efficiently. Both hands work independently, the entire process seems casual and haphazard, and it's over in seconds. Even if the cheat can do nothing more than stack one or two aces, he'll come out ahead in the long run.

In addition to stacking from the faceup board, the cheat can stack from the facedown discards that come his way prior to his deal. This is called *cull stacking*. Culling from the discards has already been described; what the cheat does here is keep track of the location of valuable cards within the discards and manipulate them to the desired position. For example, the cheat glances at a folded hand and sees that it contains a king. Simply by toying with the facedown cards, shuffling them one at a time from the top of the packet to the bottom, the cheat positions the king with the correct number of spacer cards on top, so it will fall to his hand on the deal. If more spacer cards are needed, the cheat adds them from the next set of discards. If another king shows up, the process is repeated. Irrelevant cards are slid to the bottom of the discard pile. Any final adjustments are made during the shuffles (see "False Riffle Shuffles," the 7th Way, for how to add or subtract cards from a stack). This may seem like a glaringly obvious way to stack a hand. And it is. But it makes no difference if no one is paying attention.

Prevention and Detection

Pickup and discard stacks can be assembled very quickly, and with an air of nonchalance that belies the fact that order is being imposed on seeming chaos. Most of the time all the cheat is looking for is trips or a high pair, or sometimes just a single card. To spot this kind of cheat, watch how the board is cleared. Is it done in sections, rather than all at once? Are some cards used to scoop up other cards? This is a natural action, but it's also a very efficient way to position a wanted card under a group of irrelevant cards.

Take note of the player who habitually drops out before his deal and aggressively goes after the deadwood. Does he toy with the discards, changing their order? As noted earlier, culling procedures often go unnoticed because they take place out of frame. The same is true for these stacking procedures. The more you pay attention to what goes on *between* hands, the better the chances of catching this kind of thief.

12

MARKED CARDS—AN INTRODUCTION

They read 'em. You weep.
—Frank Garcia

Marked cards—also known as *paper* and *readers*—are responsible for stealing more money than all other cheating methods combined. They're easy to use, require no sleight of hand, are readily available, and will fool anyone unfamiliar with the particular system in use. Cards can be marked on the fronts, the backs, and the edges; the work can be blended into the back design, the hue of the ink, or the feel and finish of the card. Information can be hidden in tiny spaces or sprinkled like magic dust across the entire back of a card so that it can be read from across the room. And that's just for starters.

This is a huge topic, overflowing with ingenious and unexpected ideas (Hey, let's mark the cards with radioactive iodine!). Before diving into the details, we'll start by looking at a few general principles. Subsequent chapters will dish the dirt on codes, camouflage and methods.

The Advantages

1. Marked cards allow the cheat to realize his ruling mantra: *Know thy opponent's hole cards.* This is the number-one use of marked cards. It turns poker from a game of incomplete information into one of complete information, like chess. The cheat can study both sides of the board before making his move. This is the strongest advantage a player can have.
2. Marked cards facilitate the scam known as "second dealing." The marks allow a crooked dealer to identify the top card without having to literally peek at it (his other option). If he wants it for his own hand, he keeps it in place and deals the second card instead.

3. Readers let the dealer preview the card that will fall to the first player in the *upcoming* round. If the cheat's partner is on the receiving end, the cheat will tip the card with a signal. If a rival is about to improve, the cheat can drop out rather than invest in the round of betting. Or he might tack in the opposite direction and raise, hoping to drive out the opposition and send the card where it will do no damage.

4. Finally, marked cards provide a huge edge in a variety of home games like Cincinnati, and Southern Cross, in which several community cards are dealt facedown in the center of the table, then turned over one at a time, with a round of betting after each. With paper in play, the cheat can foresee his best possible hand before a single card is turned.

Marking Strategies   There's no need to mark all of the cards to win most of the money. Often, all the cheat cares about are the high cards. Some systems mark the 10s, jacks, queens, kings, and aces with an *identical mark*, while the rest of the cards are left unmarked. This is called a two-way combination (high/other) and is the standard system for blackjack. For poker, most paper players prefer a four-way combination: the queens, kings, and aces are *uniquely marked* and the rest of the deck remains unmarked. Some cheats mark for "suit and size," and others for size (rank) alone. The fewer cards marked, the less chance of discovery. However, that doesn't rule out the use of a fully marked deck. It's cheater's choice.

Ditto for size and location of the marks. Size usually—but not always—determines the distance at which the cards can be read. Second-dealers need to see the marks close-up, in which case they are usually camouflaged in a small design element in the card's back pattern, often near the left edge. This allows the cheat to push the top cards slightly to the right and "read" the cards below it as well. To read hole cards at a distance, however, the cheat will use a marking system like "juice," where the marks are large but nonetheless invisible to the untrained eye (see the 14th Way, "Shade and Flash").

Getting the Deck Into Play   There are many sneaky ways to introduce marked cards in a private game. A simple strategy is to arrive with a couple of marked decks that have been resealed in their prophylactic cellophane and set them down near the poker table before the game even starts (see the 20th Way, "Skinning the Deck"). Eventually someone will break open a deck, and no one will question or remember where it came from. If the cheat is the host, the deck can be on the table from the start.

Paper can also be switched in midstream. The cheat knows from past games what brand of cards will be used; he brings a matching marked deck and switches it on his deal (see the 50th Way, "Deck Switches"). When the cheat has a partner at the table, switching is child's play. One cheat distracts, knocking over a pile of chips, as the other makes the switch. At the end of the night, the original deck can be switched back in, leaving no evidence. If the cheat wants to go the extra mile (many miles, actually), he can arrange it so that the *victim* of the scam provides the marked deck himself (see the 47th Way, "Papering the Neighborhood").

Marking Cards During Play   A deck that starts out honest may not end up that way. There are many, many systems for marking cards on the fly, involving nicks, pricks, crimps, waves, and daub. Any type of card can be marked with the appropriate system: casino cards, logo cards, airline cards, Bees, Bicycles, paper, or plastic. This topic is fully explored in later entries.

Selective Use   Just because the cards are marked doesn't mean the cheat will use his advantage on every hand. Too much staring at the cards is suspicious. Cheats pick their spots, going after the big pots and letting other players win the small ones. Sometimes the cheat never looks at the marks. Instead, the cards are read by one or more partners who signal the cheat what he needs to know. Often, only one player is targeted—the one with the tallest stack.

Prevention and Detection

The first line of defense against paper in public card rooms is
to shield your hole cards. In stud games, slip the pocket cards under an up card. In hold 'em, keep the pocket cards flush and pin
them with a chip stack. In draw, avoid spreading the cards in a
wide fan. While this is no guarantee—the cards can be read before
they're dealt, or *on the way over*—it sure beats leaving the cards
exposed.

In home games the best defense is to provide your own cards.
Use quality, name brand cards, and open the cards in front of the
other players. Once the game starts, protect your hole cards as described above, lest they be marked during the game.

Scouring the deck for marks is usually the *last* step in ferreting
out paper. The all-important first step is recognizing the tells that
marked cards may be in use: Is someone playing *as if* they can see
your hole cards? In a heads-up game, does the opposition fold
whenever you've got a powerful pocket pair? Or suppose you
show J-Q-K-A on the board, and lose to a guy who calls your
bluff with a pair of deuces. Lucky guess? Maybe once or twice.
But when the same player consistently wins with illogical play—
calling when he should fold, folding when he should raise—*some*
form of cheating is probably going on. It may not be marked
cards, but when other methods are ruled out, paper is a very good
guess.

Unfortunately, there is no surefire protection against marked
cards. No matter how many marking systems you know, there's
another one out there that can beat you. Guaranteed.

P.S.: The use of radioactive iodine to identify cards is tipped in
Steve Forte's magnum opus *Casino Game Protection—A Com-
prehensive Guide*. "Minute amounts of radioactive iodine have
been put on plastic cards, sealed with a matte finish, and read
through the table with dosimeters strapped to both knees. A rapid
tick-tick-tick sound was heard in an earpiece that signaled the
presence of the marked card."

A VERY BRIEF HISTORY OF MARKED CARDS

The earliest European playing cards were by their nature marked cards. Dating from the late fourteenth century, early decks were handmade, one card at a time, and then painted front and back. Discrepancies in color, design, paint texture, and the shape and cut of the cards were inevitable, allowing the shrewd observer to keep track of favorite cards.

Block printing, introduced in 1423, created a uniform look to the backs and forced cheats to come up with their own marking systems. Cardano describes several approaches, including indenting the edges, adding color to the back, roughing or polishing the surface, and creating "slight imprints with a knife."

For a short time, it seemed to manufacturers that an all-white back would discourage card markers, since any marks, smudges, or alterations would be apparent. Cheats marked the cards anyway, applying transparent varnish in a series of dots and dashes to indicate suite and value. The marks were invisible to the uninformed but could be seen by the cheat who noticed how light reflected off the marks. When manufacturers began glazing the cards, cheats countered by polishing or removing the glaze to create the same dots and dashes, or by adding thin coats of paraffin to change how the light reflected.

The battle veered off in a new direction when manufactures introduced intricate back designs featuring cross-hatching, plaids, and elaborate floral patterns. The cheats' answer was to print counterfeit decks that copied the manufacturers' designs but included a hidden "key" that identified the face of each card. These so-called stamped decks appeared in the early 1830s. The cards were poor imitations of the real thing (the inks and paper didn't always match the authentic cards), but they served the purpose for the next 30 years, until the burgeoning cheating-supply industry came up with a new innovation.

Rather than *imitate* the manufacturer's cards, the crooked gambling supply house began selling *authentic* decks that were meticulously hand marked—often by a staff of Asian women skilled in penmanship—and then resealed. These marking systems typically involved adding or subtracting details from the back design or subtly altering the color. This era thrived for more than a hundred years, until an antiracketeering crusade in the early 1960s forced most of the suppliers out of business. At the time it was estimated that 100,000 marked decks were sold annually.

Today, most professional cheats mark their own cards, as the best of them always have, using the tried-and-true systems of the past five centuries. For the amateur, Internet merchants have replaced the cheating-supply houses as the primary source for store-bought readers. Magic dealers also carry marked decks "for entertainment purposes only." Among the best are the Bicycle Rider Back decks manufactured by the U.S. Playing Card Company and sold under several different names. In theory, these cards are the ultimate "stamped deck," looking in every way like the real thing because they *are* the real thing. Fortunately for the honest player, the marks are easily detected using the riffle test explained in the following chapter.

13

BLOCKOUT AND CUTOUT WORK

No playing card in the world is immune to card marking. None!
—Steve Forte

Blockout and cutout are graphic techniques used to add an identifying "key" to the back of a playing card. The techniques are versatile and can be used on any type of back, from the most florid to the most basic. Blockout work *adds* color to the white area of a card, effectively "blocking out" any design element, or portion thereof, that appears in white. Cutout work *subtracts* color with the aid of a scalpel or X-acto knife, allowing the original white area underneath to show through. The techniques are used to lengthen or shorten lines, shrink or enlarge geometric patterns, and alter ornaments such as scrolls, arabesques, and floral designs.

This is painstaking work, requiring many hours to mark a single deck. The work was pioneered by the cheating-supply industry of bygone days, which also sold the required dyes, inks, pens and ultrafine brushes for do-it-yourselfers. A staggering number of marking systems were devised for all major brands of cards. Here we'll look at examples of the work on two popular backs, the Bicycle Rider and the Bee 67.

In the following illustration on page 46, the Bicycle card on the left was marked by yours truly and contains more marks than would normally be found on a single card. The card on the right is undoctored.

Note that in these systems, the cheat knows exactly where to look for the marks because they are always in the same location (and at both ends of the cards). Not so with the Bee card on page 47. Here the marks—which consist of tiny alterations to the red

A. Notice that several birds have been inked out using blockout work. As there are fourteen birds to choose from, theoretically the cheat can indicate the value of any card by erasing a corresponding bird. In actual practice, cheats who use this system block out only a few birds to indicate high cards.

B. The mountain is now snowcapped, the result of cutout work done with a needle. This is an example of "strong work," meaning that it is bold and can be read at a distance. What the mark signifies is, of course, up to the cheat, but this certainly is a quick and easy way to mark the aces.

C. Here a tiny bit of ornamental line has been blocked out. This is all that's needed in a two-way combination deck in which only the high cards are marked with an identical key. The mark is subtle, for the dealer's eyes only.

D. Many back designs incorporate petal-like arrangements that can be used as a clock face to indicate the value of the card. The petal corresponding to the value of the card can be narrowed, shortened, or erased altogether. The blocked-out wedge shapes can be used to signify ten through ace.

and white diamonds—are located in different positions along the length or top of the card. The *location* of the mark indicates the value. If the suit is keyed, the information is signified by which *facet* of the diamond has been altered. Reading these cards is maddeningly difficult at first. The descriptions and illustration below come from the final K.C. Card Co. catalog, issued in 1961. The marking system itself was created shortly after Bees appeared on the market in 1892.

K.C CARD CO.   / CHICAGO / WEbster 9-3515

34

READERS

Card work is one of our specialties. Our work has been recognized for years as the most perfect ever produced. All work done by experienced artists and our combinations are original and well placed.

Our ink blends perfectly and we guarantee our work to be the best obtainable. All combinations listed on the following pages are carried in stock for immediate shipment.

We will reproduce your Private Combination at an additional charge of $1.00 per deck above catalog prices if samples are submitted. We can also work out Special Combinations for you on any back. FULL REMITTANCE MUST BE SENT WITH ALL ORDERS FOR SPECIAL COMBINATIONS.

READERS BEE 67

A. Enlarged Diamonds. This is one of the best combinations on Bee 67. Placed all in the left-hand side this work cannot be improved upon. We also make this in a combination across the top or on the right hand side. [The diamond is swollen by blocking out the part of the white borders. The cheat scans the edge of the card to see which diamond has been enlarged. This keys the value.]

B. Small White Diamonds. This is similar to enlarged diamonds, but instead of enlarging red or blue diamonds, we reduce the white diamonds.

C. Double Line Work shows to better advantage than single line work. This is the old reliable, well-liked, and a better quality of work no one has been able to duplicate.

D. One side of the white diamond is reduced. Some customers prefer this to small white diamonds. The work is sometimes called Neostyle.

E. A side combination. Fine for side-dealing box.

F. Two sides of the red or blue diamond made wider. Some prefer this to Enlarged Diamonds. Reads from Ace to 7, or Ace to 2, as desired.

G. Points. Large and easy to read. Very well liked by certain of our customers.

Detection and Prevention

Virtually all forms of cutout and blockout work can be detected by the *riffle test,* also known as "taking the deck to the movies." Hold the deck firmly in one hand by the lower half, and with the other hand riffle the cards off the ball of the thumb. At the same time, focus on a small area of the back pattern, such as the birds on the Rider back. If there is "work" in the area, it will become apparent as the birds disappear, reappear and fly around like the cartoons in a flipbook.

To be thorough, you must repeat the test many times, each time focusing on a different area of the card. Check out both ends of the deck as well as the sides. What you're looking for is any design element that jumps around. If only a few cards are marked and the marks are subtle, they are easily missed.

One of the challenges of blockout work is to find an ink or dye that perfectly matches the ink on the card. This is not easy. Some cheats mark with Sharpies, but the color discrepancies can be detected by examining the card from different angles. Cutout work can also be detected by the scars it leaves on the finish of the card.

Despite the relative ease of detection, blockout and cutout work have been used to haul off truckloads of cash. The work can still turn up anytime, anyplace.

14

SHADE AND FLASH

S hade and flash are subtle card-marking systems that tell their secrets quickly, and from a distance. Picture ten players at the table, a facedown card in front of each. The uninitiated stare at their cards and see nothing; no hints from below, no hands waving in the air, no clues at all about what those cards might be. But to the cheat—to the cheat all hands are on deck, semaphores flashing strings of code: *Ace here! King! Jack!*

What the cheat sees that no one else can see is a subtle difference in color. Some area of the card has been treated to appear ever so slightly darker or lighter than it should be. The work can appear in a design element, such as a leaf or flower, or it can reveal itself to the cheat's trained eye in the form of lines, circles, dots, and dashes, depending on the back pattern and the cheat's coding system. Of all the marking systems out there, this is the method employed by the most sophisticated cheats.

Shade   When an area of the card is darkened, the work is known as shade. Tinting formulas differ according to the chemist, but the basic ingredients are a few drops of red or blue aniline dye (or ink) diluted with grain alcohol. The solution is applied with a brush or pen and imparts a faint tint to the white area of the card without altering the surrounding red or blue background.

A typical example is the "angel shade" deck (Fig. 1) in which the cheat tints one or more of the corner cherubs on a Bicycle Rider back deck to indicate the card's value. For most poker purposes, the cheat cares about only the high cards. A tinted cherub in the upper left and lower right might indicate an ace (exaggerated for clarity in the illustration); the upper right and lower left, a king; two on the same end, a queen. Systems vary.

Fig. 1

To create lines (*line shade*), the cheat carefully inks in existing white lines, such as the diagonal lines on a Bee deck. Lines can be continuous or broken (*highway shade*), and can run vertically, horizontally, or diagonally, depending on the back pattern. Because of all of the variation possible, any value can be coded without much difficulty. The hard part for the cheat is learning to see the work.

Card mechanics practice for weeks, months, or years to master a difficult sleight. Shade readers hone their skills by weaning themselves on progressively lighter and lighter hues until they can detect minute differences in tint that are completely lost on the rest of us. According to Steve Forte, shade workers have been known to take a photographer's light meter into the card room where they plan to cheat, measure the light, and then practice at home under identical conditions.

Flash   The opposite of shade is flash. In this system, the cheat tints the entire back of the card *except* for a small area which then stands out like a sore white thumb. Applying flash is much more work than marking cards with shade, but the payoff is that the marks are brighter and pop from a distance of up to ten feet, making this a preferred system for reading hole cards from across the table.

The Bee card in Fig. 2 was made by tinting the entire back except for two diamonds in diagonally opposite corners. To the cheat's practiced eye, these will blink like a neon sign. Like shade, flash can appear as lines, circles, or dots and dashes, depending on the back design. To apply flash to plastic cards, such as Kem and Copag, the cheat protects the target area with a template, then sprays the tint on with an airbrush. On paper cards, the target area is covered with masking tape or rubber cement, and the tint is brushed on. When the cover is removed, the area underneath appears brighter. As with shade, the more subtle the tint, the more difficult it is to read.

Fig. 2

Detection and Prevention

Most players today know nothing about shade or flash, even though the method has been exposed many times, going back to Robert-Houdin and Maskelyne's *Sharps and Flats* (1894). Shade decks are sold openly on the Internet and can obviously do damage in home games, provided the user puts in the practice to master the techniques involved. (I bought a deck to check out the work and have no idea whether I was ripped off or the cards actually were marked. I couldn't see a thing.) The greater danger, however, lies in underground poker clubs where the house provides the cards and who knows how many of the regulars are practiced cheats. The work has also been detected in casino settings from time to time.

Shade and flash are not susceptible to the riffle test, and trying to find the marks is difficult, especially if you have no idea where to look. Try examining the cards from various angles. A line that is invisible from one point of view may reveal itself from another. If you can manage to leave the game with a questionable deck, try exposing the cards to black light, which will cause the marks to fluoresce. This is standard practice in the casino industry whenever marked cards are suspected.

Shade can sometimes be spotted by dealing the cards rapidly while focusing on a small area of the deck, looking for a subtle shift in color. The same test sometimes works at arm's length. First impressions count. The more you look the less you see.

Flash is best spotted from a distance. Try squinting, and throwing your eyes out of focus to make the marks appear. Covering hole cards with an up-card is a strong defense against many marking systems, but not flash. Skilled readers see the marks *as the cards hit the table*.

Remember, the strongest indication that marked cards might be in use is the player who consistently makes all the right calls and laydowns. If someone is playing like they can see through your cards, maybe it's time to leave.

JUICE

Juice is a type of shade characterized by large marks that can be read from six to ten feet away but are invisible to the uninitiated. The system was developed by an anonymous sharp in the mid-1960s but remained top secret until word leaked out to the magic community in the early 1980s. Like so many once-precious secrets, it is now fairly common knowledge.

Esoteric formulas and secret ingredients are still part of the lore of juice; however, a simple form of the substance can be made by mixing the ink from a ballpoint pen or Magic Marker with grain alcohol. The solution is applied with a Q-Tip or dropped directly onto the back of the card with an eyedropper and immediately blotted up.

Typical marks include circles about the size of a dime or a quarter, and bars or dashes (Fig. 3). Juice works best on all-over backs like Bees and is read in the same way as shade, by unfocusing the eyes. Despite the size of the marks, the work is subtle and can be read only after considerable practice (the marks in the illustration are greatly exaggerated for clarity). An exposure of the system can be seen in the movie *Shade*.

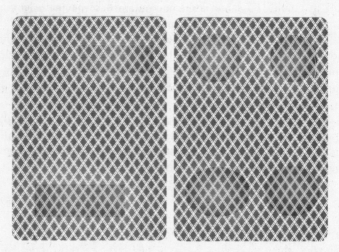

Fig. 3

15

SORTS

*One week spent on a deck of sorts will guarantee
months and months of winnings.*
—John Scarne

Sorts are, essentially, marked cards without any marks. The cards are exactly as they come from the factory. No blockout or cutout work, no shade or flash. Yet the cheat can glance at his opponents' hole cards across the table and instantly spot the aces.

The secret is an ingenious concept that takes advantage of natural variations that occur in the manufacture of playing cards. A Bee deck printed in April, for example, will not always be identical to one printed in September. And this goes for all brands of cards and all seasons. The differences can be subtle or obvious and have mainly to do with the color of the back, the uniformity of the borders, and the point at which the printed design bleeds off the edge of the card. The latter two variations occur during the "stamping" process, as individual cards are cut from a larger sheet, and are apparently inevitable.

Cheats noticed this lack of uniformity a long time ago and promptly figured out ways to exploit it. A quick and easy application, for example, is to switch the aces from a deck with equal-size borders with the aces from an unevenly cut deck (Fig. 1). Either deck can be used in the game and as a result the discrepant cards stand out like crows in a snowbank.

Rather than switching the aces, the cheat can transpose the 10s and picture cards, creating a powerful tool for cheating at blackjack. By noting the size of the borders, the cheat immediately knows if there's a ten-value on top of the deck. This is, obviously, a huge advantage in deciding whether to "hit" or stay, and can also be used to try to bust the dealer. For poker purposes, this type of two-way combination deck is used in razz and lowball to identify high cards in an opponent's hand.

Three-, four-, and five-way combination decks (such as A-K-

Fig. 1: The card on the left has uniform borders. The card on the
right, from a different print run, has unequal borders at
the short end.

Q-J-other) can be assembled using the same system, provided the
cheat can round up enough mismatched decks. In the boom times
of the cheating-supply business, combination decks were mass-
produced by sorting through tens of thousands of decks (thus the
term *sorts*), and any type of combination could be custom or-
dered. Today, it's strictly a do-it-yourself job and is considered
more trouble than it's worth.

The same type of edge discrepancies apparent on bordered
cards also exist on borderless cards such as Bees and Steamboats.
One batch of Bee decks, for example, may have been cut so that
the diamonds on the long edge are bisected, resulting in a pattern
of half-diamonds running down the length of the card, whereas
another batch will show full diamonds in the same location. The
same lack of uniformity can also be found along the short ends.
These cards require hawk-eyed vision to read at a distance but are
ideal for the dealer's eyes.

Color variations are far less common than border discrepancies but they do exist. However, rather than compare hundreds of

decks to find them, cheats used to create their own color sorts by placing key cards in the sun for several days, causing the backs to fade to a paler shade of red or blue. This was called *sunning the deck* and a lot of money was won this way. My own recent experiments, however, produced no results and my guess is that there's now some kind of UV protection built into the inks or the finish of the cards—perhaps for just this reason.

On the other hand, border sorts can be created artificially by cutting a sliver from the edge of the card, and rerounding the corners. This will, of course, change the point at which the back pattern runs off the edge of the card, making it readable and allowing for various combinations. Over-all backs are trimmed on opposite sides so the card can be read from any orientation; bordered cards can be identified when trimmed on one side only. These cards are known as *trims*. Strictly speaking, these aren't sorts— the variations aren't natural and no cards are transposed—but the cards are read in the same way.

One last method of altering the cards without literally marking them is ironing. In *Marked Cards and Loaded Dice*, Frank Garcia says that steam-ironing target cards will dull the finish and make them easy to pick out. I experimented with several brands and succeeded only in yellowing the borders. A far more workable application, revealed for the first time in Steve Forte's *Casino Game Protection*, is ironing plastic cards—in particular Kem cards. Forte calls the work the *flex*. The heat breaks down the finish and makes the treated cards more flexible. "An aggressive dealing style," says Forte, "where each card is flexed as it's dealt, is used as each top card is pitched. During the deal, the rigidness of the unmarked cards, and the softness of the marked cards proved to be an easy distinction." The dealer is in a position to know where all the high cards are and can signal his partners accordingly.

Detection and Prevention

You can't scrutinize every new deck for secret marks. There are too many marking systems and no logical place to start looking. What you can do, however, is ribbon spread every fresh deck and check for variations in color and border size. This takes only a few seconds and is standard practice in casinos and public card rooms.

If suspicion falls on the deck after the fact, there are a couple of ways to test for sorts and trims. With borderless cards, square the deck and examine one of the long sides. Because of the way the ink runs to the edge of the card, there will be a pattern of stripes or bars across the thickness of the deck. Look for irregularities in the pattern, such as a missing segment within a stripe, or a segment of white inside a red or blue stripe. These can indicate the presence of cards from another deck. You can, of course, compare the cards one by one.

To check for trims, hold the pack lightly by the ends and tap one of the long sides on the table several times. This will cause any trims to settle and reveal themselves as thin lines across the *upper* length of the deck, where the trim is recessed. Repeat the test on the short end of the deck. You can also riffle the short end with a thumb. If trims are present you may hear a soft click as the short cards flip by.

16

LUMINOUS READERS

Thanks to the colorful characters on televised poker, nobody thinks twice about sitting down at the table with guys in goofy shades and wraparound Ray-Bans. A few years ago, that was not so. Sunglasses were an instant tip-off to anyone who knew about the secret marks that were literally painted onto the backs of the cards—marks instantly visible to anyone wearing red-tinted lenses. And lots of people did know, since the method was advertised in novelty catalogues and comic books.

For those who never pored over this type of kiddy literature, luminous readers are not the sunglasses or the cheats who wear them. They're the cards themselves. When emerald green ink is applied to the red area of a red-backed card, the ink green is virtually invisible. However, when viewed through a ruby-red filter, the marks jump out—turning the card into a "reader," that is, a marked card.

Twenty-five years ago, only a nitwit would have tried to get away with readers in a real game, but luminous technology has improved. Today, a cheat can read the marks through tinted contact lenses (known as *pink eye*), or sunglasses that appear to be gray, green, or black, but have a red filter built in. In fact, in some applications, it's no longer necessary to wear shades at all. The luminous marks* can be picked up by a hidden video camera with a red filter, and the data relayed to the cheat by his offstage partner, using simple electronics. I'm not making this up. People do this.

---

*Luminous readers are not actually luminous in the sense that they generate light. It's the combination of green on red that creates a strong contrast. The green ink absorbs part of the red spectrum while reflecting all other wavelenghts, and the red filter blocks all frequencies except red. The result is that the marked area appears quite dark against the background. The same thing happens when a yellow highlighter is applied to a blue-backed card and viewed through a blue filter, although green on red is the preferred combination among cheats.

Cheats were cashing in on the basic principal by the late 1800s, and by the early 1900s onward the cheating-supply industry was promoting a full line of luminous products, including marked decks, inks, pencils, daub, glasses, and tinted visors (Fig. 1). Apart from more sophisticated filters, the tools of the trade haven't changed much, but some of the marking systems have. The old store-bought decks were often marked like football jerseys with a bold J, 9, K, A writ large across the back of the card. Current systems are more subtle. A marking code might consist of one or more thin lines, created by inking a sequence of red diamonds on a Bee card. The position of the lines indicates the value of the card. According to David Malek, an expert on luminous work, the marks can be so faint that even those wearing the glasses will find it impossible to locate them unless directed to the spot. With practice, however, the cheat can read them instantly.

As for the hidden camera and other high-tech improvements, a Web search will turn up several purveyors of luminous products (as of this writing, the asking price for a pair of gimmicked aviator-style glasses is $2,500). One entrepreneur has also come up with this wrinkle: For the cheat who normally wears prescription contacts, part of the optical filtering system can be built into the contact lenses, and the remaining part into the sunglasses. That way, even if another player happens to put on the shades, the marks on the cards remain invisible.

Detection and Prevention

One way to protect your game against luminous readers is to examine all red-backed decks through a red filter. Since you can't actually do that, the next best step is to remain alert for the indicators that marked cards may be in use. Is another player consistently playing *as if* he can see your cards? Is he calling when, logically, he should fold, or folding when he should stay in? If so—is he wearing sunglasses? Do the cards have red backs? At the very least, change to a blue-backed deck.

K·C CARD CO. / CHICAGO / WEbster 9-3515

42

LUMINOUS READERS

Luminous Readers originated and introduced by us have been successfully used in all parts of the country. These cards do not bear any visible mark, but when viewed with our Luminous Visor or our Luminous Glasses the work appears as plain as the figure 8 on the back of the cut pictured. Luminous Readers are supplied in any back, red cards only. You must have luminous glasses or visor to be able to read this work.

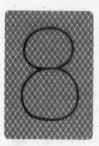

No. 888. Luminous Readers, any back . Sample Deck **$ 3.50**
　　　　Six Decks $20.50 . . . . Per Dozen **40.00**

LUMINOUS GLASSES OR VISOR

Special Glasses or Visor is necessary to read Luminous Readers and we supply whichever is best suited to your requirements.

No. 889. Luminous Glasses, for reading Luminous Readers . . . . . . Per Pair **$3.50**
No. 889-A. Clip-on Glasses to fit over your own glasses . . . . Pair **3.50**
No. 889-B. Be-Bop Style Luminous Glasses . . . . Pair **8.00**
No. 890. Luminous Visor, for reading Luminous Readers . . . . Each **3.50**

Many of our customers have been asking for a better quality Luminous Glass so we have developed a new style frame in both Ladies' and Men's special styles. Made of the finest materials available these frames help to disguise the fact that the lenses are red. Order yours today.

No. 889-L. Ladies' Luminous Glasses . . . . Pair **$12.50**
No. 889-M. Men's Luminous Glasses . . . . Pair **12.50**

LUMINOUS MATERIAL

For the operator who wishes to produce his own Luminous Readers we supply the original Luminous Marking Material, full strength, with simple complete instructions for applying. One order of our Luminous Material is enough to make 12 dozen decks or more of cards, which may be used with either our Luminous Glasses or Luminous Visor described above.

No. 666. Luminous Material with instructions . . . . Each **$5.00**

LUMINOUS INK

For those who prefer Ink to make their own Luminous Readers instead of Luminous Material we supply the original Ink, full strength. Brush for applying and complete instructions with each bottle.

No. 670. Luminous Ink for marking several gross cards . . . . Per Bottle **$5.00**

LUMINOUS DAUB

Luminous Daub is designed for use on cards and is entirely satisfactory. Cannot be seen without the use of Luminous Glasses or Visor described above.

No. 667. Luminous Daub with instructions . . . . Per Box **$3.50**

A deposit of ½ must be sent with all orders.

Fig. 1

17

MARKING CARDS IN PLAY

Here we'll look at how hustlers mark cards on the fly by nicking, bending, sanding, and otherwise mutilating them during the course of play. The strategy is simple: Mark the high cards and track their progress. Who's got them? Who's going to get them? Where are they?

Bending and Crimping   The easiest way to mark a card during the game is to bend it. Amateurs attack the corners, turning them up or down in combinations to indicate aces, kings, and queens; professionals favor less obvious systems. Often the work is nothing more than a barely discernible hump—a tiny speed bump impressed on the long side of the card, made by gently squeezing the edge of the card between the thumb and the middle and index fingers. The bend is usually put in as the cheat looks at his hole cards (Fig. 1).

The strategy is known as *playing the bend*. Usually, only the high cards are marked, and the location of the bend indicates the value of the card. A bend near the upper left corner might indicate an ace; a slightly lower bend, a king; slightly lower, a queen; and so forth. Suits are generally ignored. Whenever possible the cheat will try to

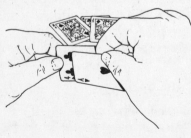

mark both the left and right edges so the card can be read across the table no matter how it is oriented. The system can reach high levels of sophistication with a bend imprinted into *any* area of the card, including the center. A trick to spotting an edge bend from afar is to look for the

Fig. 1

shadow it casts on the table, rather the bend itself (Fig. 2).

Fig. 2

Playing the bend is considered one of the safer marking systems. If the bends are discovered there's no saying who put them in, or even if they're intentional; after a while they often flatten out, leaving no evidence that marked cards were used.

Nail Nicking In this approach, also called *rim jagging, nail pricking, indexing,* and *punctuation,* the cheat vaccinates the target cards by pressing a thumbnail into the edge of the card, creating a tiny indentation. As above, the location of the mark along the length of the card indicates the value, and only a few high cards are hit ("Nick the high ones," goes an old cheaters' slogan, "and nix on the rest.")

Nicked cards are read in the same way as bent cards, but offer a bonus application. During his own deal, the cheat can glance at the side of the deck and see the whereabouts of all the cards he has marked so far (Fig. 3). If a nicked card lies far down in the pack, the cheat immediately knows that it won't come into play—always useful information. More important, he can track the progress of particular cards as they rise to the top of the deck

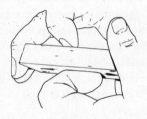

Fig. 3

during the game. When an ace or king reaches the top, the cheat knows what it is and who will get it. In a hold 'em scenario, he may also be able to identify a card when it is second, third, or fourth from the top, allowing him to foresee the turn or river cards, or part of the flop. Though the marks are small, an expert can spot them in an instant.

Edgework Here the cheat uses a fingernail to scrape some of the grime from the edge of the card. If the deck has been in play for a while, the result will be a bright white dash. This mark can be tracked in the deck like a nail nick, or read from a distance. Because the mark is bold and easy to spot, it can also be used to cull and stack. For example, if the four aces are edge marked the cheat can easily spot one when assembling the pack for his deal. As he begins the first shuffle, the cheat cuts all the cards above the ace to the right, so that the ace is the top card of the left packet. The halves are riffle-shuffled together so that the ace falls last. The deck is squared and then cut at another ace and the process repeated, adding a second ace to the first. With a few more shuffles, the aces can be stacked to fall to the cheat or his partner (see the 46th Way, "Riffle Stacking").

Sandwork Here the cheat marks the cards with a tiny square of fine sandpaper glued to his middle finger. Known as a *knockoff stick* or *sandtell stick*, the sandpaper is used, like the fingernail, to brighten a small area along the edge of the card. The cheat draws the cards he wishes to mark between this thumb and middle finger, applying pressure at the appropriate spots to identify the card. To onlookers, it appears as if the cheat is idly shifting cards from the top of his poker hand to the bottom while waiting for play to come around. The gimmick is sometimes worn under a Band-Aid with a slit cut into it. Sanded cards can be read from a distance, tracked as they rise through the deck, or cut to and stacked as previously described. Sandwork can also be applied to the back pattern, but this type of work is usually done at home, not during the game.

Detection and Prevention

Bends, nicks, and edgework can be discovered by carefully examining all four sides of the deck. Nail nicks can be obvious, but they can also be subtle, appearing as mere pinpricks. The marks can be made more apparent by beveling the side of the deck.

To test for bends and waves stand the pack on a long side, and hold it in place by posting an index finger on either side of the deck. Then relax pressure and see where the deck breaks open. Then do it again. If the pack keeps opening at the same location, one of the cards on either side of the break is warped. Check the deck from all four sides.

During the game, watch out for the player who checks his hole cards, then turns them around and checks them again. He may be marking both edges of the cards. Also be aware that some scammers strike preemptively. After raking in a few big hands, the cheat will suddenly "notice" that the aces are bent out of shape (and the kings don't look so good, either), and call for a new deck. The discovery comes just as another player makes a big score. It takes the heat off the cheat and can make a good guy look like the villain.

Many bends, nicks, and other irregularities in the deck are the result of natural wear and tear and not an indication of cheating. However, any worn deck should be taken out of play. The use of plastic cards prevents many of these problems.

TURNING THE TABLES

From *How to Spot Card Sharps and Their Methods* (1957), by Sidney Radner:

Nicking can be fouled up by an opposing player who knows the crooked trade and spots what is going on. A gambler named Old Nick Morey was reputedly a master hand at this. When he spotted an eager beaver using the pet trick from which Nick had gained his "nick" name, he would do some thumb work on the edges himself.

But Nick would mark the small cards like high ones and soon, his opponent would be losing at his own game, and wondering what was wrong with it.

18

PLAYING PAINT

In cheating parlance this method of marking cards on the fly is called *playing paint*. The scammer is known as an *artist* or *painter* and his medium is a powdery or pastelike substance called daub, or more casually, *cosmetics*.

Applied to the back of a card with a swipe of the finger, daub imparts a barely perceptible tint or smudge that allows the artist to identify his masterpieces later on. The system is versatile and works on any deck in any setting, including home games, card rooms, and casinos. It is used to read unprotected hole cards and the top card of the deck.

Playing paint is an ancient system and daub formulas vary according to the era and the manufacturer. Maskelyne reported this procedure from the late 1800s: "Olive oil, stearine, and camphor are incorporated in a melted condition with aniline of the required hue. The mixture is then poured out upon a level surface and allowed to cool. When cold it is worked up with the blade of a knife upon a sheet of white paper, to get rid of the superfluous oil. It is then ready for use."

Typical ingredients in use today include wax, oils, dye, colored chalk, greasepaint, soapstone, and commercial cosmetics. Daub is available in red and blue as well as silver and gold tints that harmonize with any color back and appear to the trained eye as a silver sheen or a subtle golden haze. When custom-made daub isn't available, cheats use substitutes such as rouge and eye shadow, cigar or cigarette ash, ChapStick, graphite, sweat, and dirt.

Painters typically enter a game with clean hands and "load up" from a concealed pallet during play. Hiding places are varied and clever. Some cheats pin a small container of daub under the hem of a jacket, or pack it into the recess of a button. Others hide it behind a tie or money clip, inside a book of matches, or on the bottom of a beer bottle. "A little-known method," says Darwin Ortiz in *Gambling Scams*, "is to smear some in one's hair at the temples. As the cheat pensively rubs his temples, he obtains some daub on his fingers in plain sight of the other players."

To apply the daub, the cheat lightly brushes his thumb or finger across the target area of the card. Generally, only the high cards are marked, and the marks are placed center and off-center, rather than near the edges where they are likely to be rubbed off during play. Hole cards are marked while peeking at them, upcards marked as they are turned facedown and added to the muck. Marking only the aces and kings will give the cheat a big edge in any game.

Daub is a strong concept for team cheats. Richard Marcus, in *Dirty Poker*, tells how he and his partners used an unspecified marking substance to attack a hold 'em game in a California card room. "After 15 minutes at the table, we had all four aces marked, one king, three of the queens, three jacks and all the 10s." Knowing their opponents' hole cards allowed the cheats to play loose and call virtually every hand before the flop. "The idea is to get into as many pots as possible and then hang around to the river only when you know your hand is best. You never have to bluff."

Prevention and Detection

Top-notch daub work is extraordinarily difficult to spot, especially on cards with repeating geometric designs, such as Bees. In fact, even when you *do* see the marks, the brain—or at least my brain—seems to dismiss them as an aberration of vision and not something actually *there*. Try marking a few cards very lightly with rouge or eyeliner to get a sense what the marks look like. If you see similar marks during a game, try rubbing them with a finger to see if something comes off. Although some daubs are permanent, most are not. Any deck with blemished cards should be taken out of play.

There's no way to stop a daub specialist from plying his invisible trade. The best defense is to shield hole cards, change decks often, and learn to recognize paint when you see it.

19

PUNCHWORK

Punchwork is a card-marking system that identifies cards by *feel* rather than sight. First described by Gilbert Walker in 1552—he called it "playing upon the prick"—the work consists of a small, raised bump or blister on the back of the card, created by pressing a sharp tool, such as a tack or needle, into the face of the card. The cheat reads the mark with his thumb. Because the blister is always placed in the same location regardless of the value of the card, a deck can be marked to answer only a single yes or no question. Is the card on top of the deck high or not? An ace or not? A heart or not? This information by itself is hugely profitable in many games. However, when combined with second dealing, punchwork creates a synergy that neither system has on its own: In theory, it gives the cheat the potential to deal a winning hand from a shuffled deck without ever having to peek at a card or look for marks.

Punchwork is usually put into the deck before the game. Professionals use a tool known as a card punch or pegger which is calibrated to raise the hump without penetrating the surface of the card. With care, a sewing needle or pushpin can be used. Cards can also be pegged during play using a thumbtacklike device glued to the first joint of the thumb, or by wearing a special ring with a point at the bottom. This is seldom done, however, because of the difficulty of using the device undetected, and the dangers of being caught red-handed.

Cheats will mark the cards at either outer corner, depending on preference or how the mark is to be used. If placed on the non-index corner (upper left with the cards facedown), the mark is read by the left thumb. This is the usual method. If the blister is on the outer right corner, the hump is felt by the right thumb as the card is taken and dealt. The cards are pegged on diagonally opposite corners so they can be read regardless of the deck's orientation.

Maskelyne was the first to mention the use of punched cards in conjunction with the second deal. "The sharp will prick the corners of all the aces and court cards . . . and whilst dealing, he can feel the little projection caused by the prick, and hold these cards back till they could be dealt to himself." The cheat has no idea which cards he's feeding himself; however he's virtually guaranteed to wind up with a fist full of color. A drawback to the system is that sooner or later the opposition can't fail to notice the shower

READING THE FACES

A cousin of punchwork known as *black line work* relies on marking the *faces* of the cards. As in punchwork, the cards are identified by feel. The mark is a small incision, grooved into the borders of all the picture cards with a sharp knife, adjacent to the index. The mark is read from beneath with the middle finger of the left hand as the top card is pushed over for dealing. The system is used strictly for low-ball.

The method is subtle and will frustrate any player who suspects marked cards but examines only the backs.

of kings, queens, and aces falling like answered prayers to the cheat or his partner. Some hustlers sidestep the problem by pegging medium-value cards instead, figuring that winning with trip sixes is less memorable than whacking the competition repeatedly with aces over kings. Another approach is to peg all the cards of the same suit, which enables the cheat to deal himself a flush on demand. But again, over the course of an evening the ploy has limited use.

For this reason, the most sophisticated use of punchwork is strictly for information. Simply pegging the aces is enough to give the cheat a winning edge in all stud games as well as hold 'em and Omaha. Even if he doesn't deal it to himself, he always knows who's got the proverbial ace in the hole. In a razz or low-ball scenario, the cheat gains a huge advantage by pegging the 10s and

DEALING IN THE DARK

A gambler named Shock related the following story to Dai Vernon, the great sleight-of-hand artist and connoisseur of gambling scams.

During the 1920s, a gang of punchworkers in the Midwest traveled from town to town with a locksmith in their crew. When the gambling joints closed for the night, the locksmith would break in and unlock the cabinet where the cards were kept. The gang would mark all the decks, then lock everything back up. Punchwork was the preferred marking system because the gambling houses typically operated in dimly lit backrooms and basements where deciphering visible marks was often impossible.

The following night the cheats would return to the club as customers. In those days, the deal still passed from player to player. Whenever it was a cheat's turn to deal, he'd read the marks, signal his partners, and clean up.

picture cards. As he deals around the table he keeps track of where the high cards fall and knows who's bluffing and who has the genuine lows. When a high card falls to a late position in the first betting round, the cheat will often signal his partners to check, giving the targeted player the opportunity to toss money into the pot with a futile bluff.

Using punchwork to deal a winning hand can be done only a few times a night before arousing suspicion. Playing for information can be done every hand, all night long.

Prevention and Detection

Punched cards are not difficult to detect if you know what to look for. The most obvious tell is a tiny indentation or pinprick on the *face* of the card. It's easy to see, but easy to dismiss or ignore if you have no reason to think twice about it.

On the other hand, a blister on the back of a card is difficult to see from more than a few inches away. But, of course, it can be felt. And that's basically the test for punchwork. Feel the corners of each card. If you've got bumps, you've got problems.

20

SKINNING THE DECK

Just because a deck of cards comes out of a box with cellophane and seal intact doesn't mean it hasn't been marked or messed with. Cheats have more than one way to sneak a deck of cards out of a sealed box and back in again without leaving signs of forced entry. The trick is to leave the usual point of entry intact and find another way in. The process is known as *skinning* the deck.

The work: The first step is to remove the box from the cellophane without opening the pull-strip. A very direct way is to cut a three-sided trap door into the cellophane at the bottom of the box using a scalpel or X-acto knife. The case is then slid out, leaving the wrapper more or less intact. To enter the box, the cheat slides the scalpel under the flap on one of the long sides, and draws the blade from one end to the other, breaking the glue seal. The flap, which has tabs at both ends, can now be pulled down and the cards removed and marked (Fig. 1).

Fig. 1

The cards are then re-cased, the tabs inserted under the top and bottom flaps, and the long flap is glued back in place with white glue or rubber cement. The box is slipped back into the cellophane and the trap door attached to the bottom of the box using a few dots of transparent glue, such as Krazy Glue. While cellophane resealed this way will not withstand careful scrutiny, it usually doesn't have to. Unless there is reason to suspect foul play, most players pay no attention to the bottom of the box. What counts is that the pull-strip and the manufacturer's seal are intact. Some cheats, however, go the extra mile and actually unwrap and rewrap the box without making any cuts. This is extremely difficult to do without damaging the cellophane. Quality card manufacturers, such as the U.S. Playing Card Company—makers of Bee, Bicycle, Tally-Ho, and other popular brands—use wrapping and gluing procedures engineered to thwart this kind of tampering. But, with a great deal of care, it can be done.

Prevention and Detection

It pays to examine the packaging before breaking open a new deck. The cellophane should be smooth and tight, with no extra folds or burrs. The pull-strip should be intact. Most major brands have their name printed on the strip. Check the bottom of the box for glue dots or cut marks; there shouldn't be any.

The box itself should also appear tamper free. No spots of glue along the side, no smudges, no signs of wear and tear. Examine the side flap carefully for tiny warps, bumps, or inconsistencies. Some cheats go through the top of the box rather than the side, so check the seal for signs of tampering. If it was steamed off and re-glued, there may be loose edges or other signs of foul play. Restoring an opened box to its original condition with no tells is not easy.

HOW TO INSPECT A NEW DECK

It takes only a minute to check out a new deck for signs of tampering. Begin by removing the advertising cards and jokers and ribbon-spread the deck faceup so that all the cards are visible. In major brands manufactured in the United States, the order of the cards is ace through king of hearts, ace through king of clubs, king through ace of diamonds, and king through ace of spades. If the cards are *not* in this order—and you have a deck of Bees, Bicycles, Tally-Hos, Steamboats, Aviators, or other well-known brand—something is wrong.

Next, check the orientation of the pips. The 2s, 4s, 10s, and picture cards are symmetrical—turn them 180 degrees and they look the same. The remaining cards—the 3s, 5s, 6s, 7s, 8s, and 9s—have a one-way orientation: Some of the pips on these cards will be pointing in one direction and some in the other. In a new deck, the majority of the pips on these cards should be oriented the same way as the ace of spades. In other words, if the ace points north, the majority of pips on the 9 of clubs, or the 5 of hearts, etc., should also point north. The diamond suit is an exception because the pips are symmetrical. But check the 7 of diamonds: The odd pip should be on the end of the card corresponding to the direction of the ace of spades. If any of the cards are misoriented, they may have been turned around by accident during tampering.

After inspecting the faces, spread the deck facedown and examine the backs. If the cards have borders, these should be the same size on each card. Also look for variations in color that might indicate "sorts." Finally, square the deck and examine the edges: All the cards should be identical in size and free of nicks or indentations. If the edges have a pattern, the result of an overall back design, the pattern should be uniform.

21

LOCATION PLAY

*A cheater can take all the chumps in the game simply
by knowing the location of very few cards.*
—John Scarne

Playing "location" is a little-known form of larceny that gets
the money and leaves no fingerprints. It's difficult to see it
coming and next to impossible to reconstruct after it's over. It can
be worked "single-o" or with a partner. Next to collusion, it's one
of the most undetectable scams out there.

Here's the basic idea: The cheat memorizes a small group of
cards—they can be discards, culled cards, exposed cards, flashed
cards—and tracks their progress as they're *legitimately* cut into
the deck. Now one of two things will happen; either the slug will
surface (come to the top of the deck) during the course of the
game, or it will not. Either way, the cheat has an advantage. If a
card surfaces, the cheat naturally knows what cards will follow it,
or by working backward, knows which cards have preceded it
and *who has them*. And if the slug is cut *out of play*, the cheat is
aware of several cards he cannot possibly hope to catch on the
draw—and that his opponents cannot possibly have in the hole.

This is powerful information in any form of poker. For example,
consider a hold 'em scenario in which the cheat has memorized the
sequence 8-9-10-J-Q. If the eight hits the flop—X-X-8—the cheat
knows that the turn and river cards will be the 10 and queen,
guaranteed. If the flop comes up J-Q-X, the last two seats were
dealt the 8 and 9. The scam works the same way in stud. The
fewer players in the game when the slug surfaces, the further
ahead the cheat can "see" and the greater his advantage. The information will not affect the outcome of every game, but it sure
informs the cheat how to best play his cards.

Now take this scenario: The cheat culls the four aces to the top
of the deck and keeps them in place with a series of false shuffles.
The last riffle shuffle is genuine and distributes the aces evenly in

the top quarter of the deck. Now the cutter cuts the deck about a third of the way down, effectively taking the aces out of play. Knowing that no other player can possibly have an ace is a huge advantage (the king is the "new ace"). The same holds true with random cards, although the example is not quite so dramatic. If the 2 of hearts, 7 of spades and king of hearts are out of play, those are three cards that cannot possibly make or break the game.

When the cheat has a partner at the table, the ally can do all the memory work—remembering a folded hand, for example— and the dealer's role is simply to control the cards to the top of the deck for the next deal. Following an honest cut, the cheat's part- ner will have a pretty good idea whether those cards will surface or not. Either way, he's ahead.

Finally, location can be utilized on another player's deal. Ca- sual card players often unintentionally expose the bottom few cards while shuffling. A shrewd observer can not only remember the cards, he can also track them through a series of shuffles and the final cut. An expert can tell, with an amazing degree of accu- racy, whether the cards are likely to surface, and whether they might influence his hand (by hitting the flop, for example). But is this cheating? The Renaissance mathematician and gambler Giro- lamo Cardano offered his opinion in *A Book on the Games of Chance*: "Those who know merely by close attention what cards they are to expect are not usually called cheats, but are reckoned to be prudent men." However, those who manipulate the posi- tions of those cards "carry out dangerous frauds which are wor- thy of death."

Protection and Detection

Location play is subtle and impossible to detect with certainty. Even if you were to scrutinize the deck prior to the deal, there's nothing to see. And that final, legitimate cut seems to rule out trickery.

So what do you watch for? The setup procedures that make lo- cation possible: the flashing of cards, the setting aside of discards, and the false shuffles that keep culled cards on the top or bottom of the deck.

As in all situations when manipulation is suspected, the sure-fire way to thwart the cheat is to ask for the deck and shuffle the cards yourself. This is rarely done in home games where asking to shuffle on someone else's deal is tantamount to an accusation of cheating. In fast company, however, it's a given that multiplayer shuffles are a reasonable safeguard against many forms of cheating. Usually, nobody takes it personally.

22

A SIMPLE RIFFLE STACK

This easy yet ingenious shuffle sequence provides the cheat with a huge amount of information. He knows his opponent's hole cards before they do. With luck, he can predict up-cards in any stud game. He might even peer into the future and see the flop, the turn, and the river.

If this sounds like déjà vu all over again, there's a reason. This machination delivers the identical results as a lay stack (the 4th Way); it positions a known sequence of cards—such as A-4-K-K-6-3—on top of the deck. It also has identical applications. Same destination, alternate route.

The work: This is simply a series of top card riffle-peeks (the 8th Way) that automatically stacks the deck. Card enthusiasts will enjoy playing with the move. It provides a sense of accomplishment without the practice required to *really* stack a deck—that is, set up one or two complete hands while shuffling. The following description is best understood with a deck in hand.

Split the pack in half and shuffle the packets together, using a table riffle shuffle. Time the riffles so that the last card released comes from the left packet, and glimpse and remember it as it falls (Fig. 1). Say it's a 3. Square the deck, cut the top half to the *right* and repeat the sequence. Voilà! The new peeked card, say it's a 6, *automatically falls on top of the one just remembered.* Now remember 6-3. Repeat as often as desired until you've crocheted a tidy little stack. Four shuffles are usually enough,

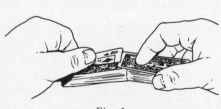

Fig. 1

although sometimes you can spot and remember *two cards* from the left packet, thereby cutting down on the number of shuffles, or increasing the depth of the stack. As with a lay stack, the selection of cards is random, but you've nonetheless assembled a bomb. As deception expert Eric Cartman would say, "Sweeeeet."

What happens next depends on, ah, what happens next. If the cheat succeeds in wiping out the obligatory cut, the most advantageous way to proceed is simply to deal the stack. It hardly matters what the game is. It's like dealing the first six or seven cards faceup.

But suppose the deck is truly cut? The cheat, having foreseen this possibility, switches to plan B and turns the stack into a location play. As the deck is cut, he estimates the size of the cut and determines if or when the stack will surface (seasoned estimators are rarely off by more than one or two cards). If the deck is cut evenly, for example, the stack will be under 26 cards and will unequivocally be *out of play* in any heads-up game. In seven-handed stud, however, the slug will reliably surface on third or fourth street, since the initial deal burns 21 cards and brings the stack sixth from the top. If many players fold, the cheat may eventually find himself facing one or two opponents with certain knowledge of the next five or six cards.

Other scenarios can easily be imagined and will vary according to the game, the number of players, where the deck is cut, who stays, who folds, and what cards are dealt. What's important is that the cheat has worked out all his options from past experience. He thinks on his feet, adapting to the situation at hand. Close-up magicians call this kind of improvisation "jazz magic." It's one of the things all tricksters do.

Detection and Prevention

The key to spotting any type of peek is to *watch the dealer's eyes*. In particular, look for a quick shift in focus down to the deck, just as the shuffle is completed. Also watch out for too many riffle shuffles that seem too measured, as if the shuffler were releasing cards in a controlled, deliberate manner. Unless this technique is done flawlessly, it's not that difficult to spot.

23

CHEATING WITH CHIPS

Thieves respect property. They merely wish the property to become their property.
—G. K. Chesterton

Fans of subtle and ingenious scams will find little to applaud in the following deceptions, which rely almost entirely on lying and stealing. For the cheat, the bottom line is to stockpile chips. These methods do so as directly as possible, no cards required.

Chip Copping This is, essentially, thievery disguised as help. When someone *other* than the cheat wins the pot, the scammer jumps right in and pushes the pile of chips toward the winner, stealing, or *copping,* a chip in the process.

There are a couple of ways to do this. The cheat starts by spotting a high-value target chip near the edge of the pot. As he shovels the chips across the table, he pins the target chip under the heel of his hand, near the base of the thumb, sliding it forward. As both hands return to home base, the heel remains in contact with the captured chip, dragging it along for the ride. The fingers remain open and spread, in a disarming display of innocence. As long as the cheat's actions are perceived as helpful, this scam will go right by.

For an extra edge, some thieves employ *chip cop*, a sticky substance applied to the palm that picks up chips like a magnet. Once a staple of gambling supply houses, cop was originally made of beeswax. Most cheats who use the stuff formulate their own, utilizing a miscellany of tacky ingredients such as hair spray, and the backing of adhesive tape that has been heated and scraped off with a knife (an old method, reported by John Scarne). The cop sticks to the palm and the chip sticks to the cop, allowing the hand to be lifted from the table, rather than slid back. A cheat will often start the game "clean" and apply the cop during a bathroom break.

Another type of thievery is to call a bet by tossing in chips that fall a bit short of the pot. The cheat then pushes them forward with cards in hand so that one of the chips rides up onto the back of the cards and is covered by the fingers as the rest of the chips coalesce with the pot. The stolen chip is then later added to the cheat's stack.

Chips can also be pilfered directly from the pot under the guise of making change, or by "helping" to divvy up a split pot, so as to speed up the game. During the course of an evening these petty thefts add up.

Splashing and Miscalling   As used by cheats, splashing is a track-covering move. Splashing refers to what happens when you *toss* chips into the pot so that they bounce and "splash" off the chips already there, making it impossible to tell how many just came in; which is the whole idea. The cheat misstates the amount of his bet and splashes the pot to cover the lie.

The most obvious approach is simply to *pretend* to toss in, say, five chips when only four are added. Unless viewed from below, the charade is well covered by the back of the hand and is surprisingly effective, especially when reinforced by a verbal declaration of the amount of the bet. Sneakier still, a cheat might openly count out the correct amount for all to see. As he adds them to the pot, however, the cheat holds back the topmost chip which is concealed beneath the fingers. The tossing arm remains in motion, first going toward the pot and immediately returning to the edge of the table where the chip is released into the lap, or added to the cheat's stack. Each time the cheat does this, the eventual winner of the pot is gypped.

Bank Robbery   In many home games, players buy chips from a designated banker and redeem them at the end of the session. In this scam, the cheat comes to the table already holding a stash of chips that match, in brand and color, those used in the game. He smuggles these into his rack. After a couple of hours, the cheat cashes in and goes home ahead of the other players. Even if he only broke even, he will automatically be ahead by the amount of chips smuggled into the game. The fraud won't be discovered until the final players try to cash out and discover the bank is short, and there are now more chips than fit in the box. If other players also left early, it's anybody's guess who the villain is. Professional cheats regard this as the lowest form of cheating.

Prevention and Detection

Lying and stealing are not difficult concepts to come up with, which is why these scams are common. However, basic housekeeping and a few sensible rules will help keep things honest.

For starters, except for the winner, it's hands off the pot. No helpful pushing of the chips, no making change, no self-appointed tenders of the pot. Also, no splashing. Bets should be neatly stacked and pushed into the pot. Or if gently tossed, as they do on TV, the chips should end up in front of the bettor, where the amount is clearly visible, and then pulled into the pot by the dealer.

If you have reason to think the pot is short, stop the game and count. Even if you don't nail the thief red-handed, checking the pot will let him know you are on to him. Thieves and miscallers often begin with honest play and only start cheating once the other players have accepted their style. Stay alert.

Some players purchase custom monogrammed chips from a gaming supply house. After you've registered your chip, no one can duplicate it. Or so they say.

INSIDE JOBS

Casinos aren't too concerned about poker players copping chips, since players must keep their mitts off the pot until it's delivered to them by the dealer. Usually, it's not the customers who are the problem—it's the help.

Employee theft is a huge problem for casinos. Anyone who comes into contact with the chips is a potential thief. Crooked blackjack dealers routinely steal by overpaying their agents at the table and splitting the boodle later. Some slip a chip under a watch band, or pop a chip into the mouth while covering a cough, a practice known as *chip monking*. An old-time method, apparently still in use today, is to palm chips and drop them into a *sub* (short for submarine), a concealed pouch sewn into the front of the pants, which the dealer opens by sucking in his gut. In fact, it is to prevent chips from "going south" that many dealers are required to wear aprons and "dust" their hands before leaving the table, exposing bare palms to the gods of surveillance.

At the poker table, corrupt dealers can enrich their coffers by copping a few extra chips while collecting the rake (the percentage of the pot that goes to the house). This is easy; generally no one is paying much attention. The house's cut is dropped through a slot in the table, and the extra chips are added to the change rack, a practice known as *padding the rack*. The dealer is now clean. Later, the rack is collected by the shift boss, who is in on the scam, and the spoils are divided. The house's percentage is never tampered with, so no red flags go up. The stolen money belongs to the winner of the hand, not the casino.

24

THE SECOND DEAL

Man: *Say, is that a game of chance?*
W. C. Fields: *Not the way I play it.*
—My Little Chickadee

Shortly after the invention of marked cards, some smart guy must have realized what an advantage it would be if, whenever an ace or other juicy card came to the top of the deck, he could deal it to himself, instead of wasting it on an opponent. But how—if the card was scheduled to go elsewhere?

The answer occurred to someone in Renaissance Italy, during the early 1500s. A Latin manuscript in the British Library that explains the deception includes no details on technique, only the observation that a cheat can deal the second card from the top of the deck *as if* it were the top card.

Today, there are two principal methods of dealing seconds, known as the *push-off* and the *strike*. Both mimic the actions of normal dealing. The left thumb pushes the top card to the right, and the right hand takes the card, thumb on top and fingers below, and deals it. At least, that's the appearance. In the push-off, not one but *two cards* are pushed to the right in close alignment. The right hand comes over as if to take the top card, but at the last moment the left thumb pulls it back, and the second card is taken instead (Fig. 1). The card can also be dealt faceup, stud style. In that case, the right

hand approaches the top card palm-down. As the left thumb pulls the top card back, the right fingers contact the second card and drag it forward, as the right thumb secures the card from beneath and helps pivot it faceup.

In the strike, the single top card is pushed to the right and slightly downward,

Fig. 1

exposing the front edge and
outer right corner of the card
beneath. This area is known
as a *brief* (Fig. 2). As the right
hand mimes taking the top
card, the right thumb
"strikes" the brief and propels
the second card diagonally
forward where it is taken be-

Fig. 2

tween the thumb and fingers, and dealt. The left thumb, meanwhile, pulls the top card back flush with the deck.

The keys to a deceptive second deal are an even dealing
rhythm, no visible tension, delicate touch, precise finger positions,
and coordinated hand motions that help blur potential tells. Also
needed: a moist thumb, warm hands, decent cards, and endless
practice.

There are many applications, but I'll limit myself to the four
most common.

The Basic Play   The cheat identifies the top card—using either a top card peek (see the 8th Way), or marked cards—and decides whether he wants it. If so, he deals "seconds" to the other
players and takes the top card for himself. He can also send it to
an ally.

Collusion   The cheat's partner signals which card or cards
he needs to improve. If the card surfaces during the deal, the cheat
holds it back, deals seconds, and sends the desired card to his
partner. Time permitting, the cheat can signal what card is on top,
and his partner can accept or decline the offer. (See the 3rd Way,
"Table Talk," for methods of signaling.)

Defense   The cheat sees that he's about to deal a third 8 to
an opponent who's already got two on the board. Instead, he
deals a second and sends the 8 to the next player.

Sabotage   The cheat can use the second deal to bust a potentially winning hand. This is especially effective in lowball

where the cheat can hold back a picture card and send it to his opponent on the draw. In razz (seven-card stud, low hand wins), the same approach can be used on the river, when two of the up-cards are in the "high zone." The cheat can even signal a partner, "Hey, this guy is about to go down in flames, stay in!"

Naturally, all of this second dealing requires more than just technical skill. A nimble "number-two man" has to be able to identify the top card, evaluate its utility, decide whether to keep it, deliver it to a partner, send it to any other player, or deal normally—all while dealing and making small talk. In most circumstances, it is strictly the first card of the round that the cheat checks out for possible use. Once he begins dealing the round, it's virtually impossible to "read" the cards and make instant decisions. The exception is punchwork, the subject of the 19th Way.

Here's a bonus application to draw poker that's worth the price of admission: Imagine a five-handed game in which, after the initial deal, the cheat is one spade short of a flush. He peeks the top card. If it's a spade, he deals seconds to *every player in the draw,* taking the spade on his own turn and making the flush. If the spade isn't there, no problem. The cheat deals honestly to the first player. As attention shifts to the two-seat, the cheat peeks at the new top card. If it's a spade he reserves it for himself; if not, he deals honestly. Working around the table in this fashion, provided that each player draws at least one card, by the time it's the cheat's turn to draw he will have had *five opportunities* to find the needed spade. And, if fortune still hasn't smiled, he can create a *sixth opportunity* by dealing himself a second, finally relying on the luck of the draw. This stratagem can be used whenever the cheat needs a single card, whether it's to fill a straight, complete a flush, or turn two pair into a full boat. Is this an advantage, or what?

Detection and Prevention

How often a skilled second dealer will actually *move* during play depends on the sophistication of the game. In fast company cheats bide their time, disarming the opposition with honest and skillful play. The legendary second dealer Irving Walter Scott kept his tools under wraps for *days* before going for the kill. Some cheats will move no more than two or three times a night, and only when the payoff is there. Among chuckleheads, however, even a mediocre deuce dealer will try to get away with murder. Here's what to look for.

Watch for a constant shuttling between the hand and mouth as the cheat moistens his thumb for better traction. This is a key tip-off. Staring at the top of the deck while dealing, and changes in the rhythm of the deal are other signs of "deuce dealing."

. Observe the dealer's thumb on the hand holding the deck. In an honest deal the thumb naturally lifts off the pack as it moves back to push over the next card. If the thumb remains glued to the top card, it's likely that seconds are being dealt. Also, eyeball the outer left corner of the top card for a telltale back-and-forth movement that shouldn't be there.

These tells are much easier to see if you are seated next to the dealer. In heads-up play across the table, the cheat will often neck-tie the deck—that is, tilt the deck inward toward the chest—so that the top of the pack is actually out of sight as the cards are dealt. This makes dealing seconds a breeze, even with less than stellar technique. Many players necktie the deck unconsciously, so don't assume the worst when you see this. Just ask that the deck be kept parallel to the table, as it's done in casinos.

Finally, there's the *sound* of the deal. Because of the friction created by the top card on the second, there is a noticeable *swish* as the second is pulled from the deck. There's no doubt it sounds different than a normal deal. Whether this difference is actually *audible* during a game, distinguishable from the attendant ambient noise, is a matter of opinion. Some experts swear they can hear it; others consider detection by *swish* to be a myth.

RESOURCES

A great way to appreciate the aesthetics of a second deal is to watch an expert deal seconds with the top card faceup. What you get is a wonderful and disconcerting illusion as your brain is assaulted with mixed signals. Past experience says you're watching a normal deal; present experience—in the form of that never-changing, faceup top card—tells you you're not. So what you "see" is facedown cards melting through the top of the deck and into the dealer's hand. It's cognitive dissonance at its finest.

For video demonstrations, check out the work of experts Richard Turner, Steve Forte, and David Malek. In the movies, magician Paul Wilson deals beautiful seconds with the ace of spaces faceup during the closing credits of *Shade*; John Scarne's second deal shows up in *The Sting* in the scene where Henry Gondorff (Paul Newman) limbers up his card chops before going into the big game against Doyle Lonnegan; and magician Jay Ose does seconds and teaches the basics of card handling to Joan Blondell in a "bonus featurette" included with *The Cincinnati Kid* on DVD.

For detailed written instruction, the following texts are recommended: Hugard and Braue, *Expert Card Technique;* S. W. Erdnase, *The Expert at the Card Table*; Bill Simon, *Effective Card Magic*; and Eddie McGuire, *The Phantom of the Card Table.*

25

THE BOTTOM DEAL

*If requested to determine from what single artifice
the greatest advantage is derived, we would
unhesitatingly decide in favor of bottom dealing.*
—S. W. Erdnase

Dealing from the bottom of the deck offers the poker cheat several advantages over other sleights and swindles. Among them: the ease of gathering and retaining wanted cards on the bottom of the pack until needed; the flexibility of dealing the cards on any round to any position; the elimination of any stacking procedures to produce a winning hand; and the ease of overcoming the cut thanks to a unique strategy that requires no partner, no crimping, and no reversing of the cut packets. For top mechanics over the centuries, the bottom deal has been the bread-and-butter move.

Before considering the applications, let's look briefly at the two main techniques. In the approach favored by Erdnase, the sleight begins as the left thumb pushes the top card to the right. A moment later, the left ring finger ducks beneath the deck and pushes the bottom card to the right, bringing it into close alignment with the top card (Fig. 1). This action is hidden by the projecting top card. As the right hand reaches for the top card to deal it, the left thumb pulls it flush with the deck and the bottom card is taken instead. "This can be done so perfectly that the quickest eye cannot detect the ruse," Erdnase comments, adding, "It requires some practice." The card can be dealt facedown, or faceup, stud style.

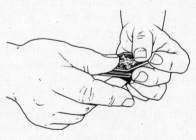

Fig. 1

In the alternate approach, the bottom card is not pushed out from under the deck. Instead, as the right thumb contacts the top card to apparently deal it, the right middle finger extends beneath the deck, entering the gap between the second and third fingers and draws out the bottom card, the left fingers opening slightly to

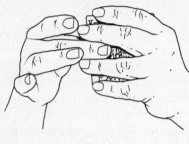

allow this (Fig. 2). The middle finger can also be inserted between the fourth finger and the pinkie instead, depending on the grip. The top card is moved back and forth to simulate a normal deal.

Each of these approaches has many variations, none of which we'll explore here other than to mention that

Fig. 2

bottoms can be dealt from a variety of grips, and that the cards can be pivoted, snapped, or smoothly drawn from the bottom of the pack, as the right hand moves to the right, forward, or diagonally.

Dealing a Winning Hand with Preselected Cards

The chief advantages of bottom dealing are directness, flexibility, and sure knowledge of what's coming. After culling a strong hand—three queens, for example—the cheat is free to deal the cards in any way he chooses, on any round, and without the bother of inserting spacer cards or resorting to any of the complex shuffling systems used to make sure the cards fall to the desired position at the table.

In a draw poker scenario, for example, the cheat will almost always deal the first round honestly, reserving the queens for the draw. There are two reasons for this: The fewer cards in the deck the easier it is to deal bottoms, and by dealing the initial cards from the top, the cheat or his partner have a 50 percent chance of getting a pair, any pair, purely by chance. Whoever gets the pair draws three, and a full boat! Who said cheaters never win?

In seven-card stud, the cheat will likely deal only a single bottom during the first round, giving his partner a queen and an x card in the hole. The second bottom can be dealt on fourth, fifth, or sixth street—dealer's choice—and the final queen arrives face-down on the river, neatly concealing the strength of the hand. Because the cheats know what's on the horizon they can, naturally, bet aggressively, and if everyone falls by the wayside the last queen is never dealt.

Bottom dealing also works in a hold 'em scenario. Local conditions permitting, the cheat will deal his partner pocket queens to start. This is not too difficult, since there will be only two bottom deals in the entire dealing round. The flop and the turn are dealt honestly and the third queen appears on the river.

Taking Advantage of Random Bottom Cards   In this application, no cards are culled to the bottom. The cheat simply peeks the bottom card (the 9th Way) at every opportunity and decides how to use it. The cheat may have a pair of queens and discover, by chance, that the bottom card is also a queen. Or his partner signals that he needs an 8 or a king to complete a 9-10-J-Q straight. If there's one on the bottom, the partner gets it. If not, the cheat deals the bottom card to another player and checks again, continuing in this fashion for several cards. In razz or hi-lo the cheat has more options, as a high-value card on the bottom can be used to improve a high hand or bust a low one. As the game unfolds, so does the strategy. Because the cheat can summon a fresh bottom card whenever he chooses, simply by dealing the existing bottom card, he will have many opportunities to influence the outcome of the game, improving or ignoring hands as he chooses.

Bonus Application—Stacking a Hand   I had never considered this surprising use of the bottom deal until Steve Forte shared it with David Britland and Gazzo, who published it in *Phantoms of the Card Table*. The method also appears in Forte's magisterial *Casino Game Protection*. It works like this: The cheat culls the target cards to the bottom of the deck—we'll stick with the queens—and then counts the cards to make sure no one is holding out (see the 30th Way, "Holding Out"). It's under the guise of counting that a stacking procedure takes place. The count begins normally, but at some point the cheat deals a bottom, followed immediately by four tops, another bottom, four tops, another bottom, and four more tops. The next card is dealt off-center, to act as a marker, and the count is completed. The cheat now picks up the deck and cuts everything below the marker card to the top of the deck. When five hands are dealt, all from the top, the dealer will have trip queens. Naturally, the set can be arranged to fall to any hand, and the system works with any number of players.

Prevention and Detection

Unless you routinely play for high stakes, chances of running into a skilled bottom dealer—AKA *base dealer*, *b-dealer*, *cellar* or *subway man*—are slim. The top mechanics work as ringers, infiltrating big-money games in big city hotels, targeting salesmen and conventiongoers, or posing as wealthy friends of the rich and famous. These guys are not after my hundred bucks, or yours.

Bottom dealing has three serious tells: "getting a hanger," "dealing air," and "finger flash." In the first instance, two cards come off the bottom instead of a single. One ends up in the cheat's hand and the other juts from the deck like a diving board. (This is the fate that befalls Worm, the subway dealer in *Rounders* played by Edward Norton, versus a crew of off-duty cops.) Dealing air means getting no card whatsoever. The hand comes away from the deck empty. Finger flash refers to the brief exposure of the left fingers or knuckles as they come away from the deck, allowing the bottom card to be drawn out. If you see any of these, head for the exit.

In some instances, how the dealer grips the pack can be a tell, since certain grips are associated with certain methods. It's also true that practice makes perfect and bottoms can be dealt from any grip at any time, given sufficient practice. Rather than watching for the grip, look for the culling process that sets up the bottom deal.

BEATING THE CUT CARD ONE MORE WAY

Professional bottom dealers almost always work with a partner who helps them beat the cut, cull the cards, and take down the big pots. When playing solo, however, the base dealer still needs a way to have the pack legitimately cut, yet end up with the slug on the bottom.

One answer is *palming*, also known as *holding out*. Just before offering the deck for the cut, the cheat squares the cards between his hands and under cover of the top hand, pivots the bottom few cards to the right and curls them into the left palm. The right hand tables the deck as the left hand turns palm-down, hiding the copped cards. Following the cut, the moves are played backward and the palmed cards are added back to the bottom of the deck as it is returned to the left hand for dealing. This ploy can be used even if a cut card is employed to foil bottom dealing. The cheat simply places the held-out cards under the cut card. At the end of the deal, everything is as it should be. (See the 33rd Way, "Cheating with the Cut Card," for another approach.)

Finally, the use of a cut card is an excellent defense against the bottom deal. It's not foolproof, but it will deter all but the most tenacious.

THE THREE BS

It takes more than technical skill to deal bottoms during a game. The other imperative is nerve. "Do you realize how much tension you are under when you have seven men looking at you?" asked the confessed cheat Walter Irving Scott. "A true cheater has to work under fire when the money is on the table and the players are all looking. Do you realize how *hard* it is to take that card off the bottom?" Or, as the old-time hustlers put it, the measure of the cheat was his mastery of the three Bs: briefs, bottoms, and balls.

26

THE CENTER DEAL

*When a cheater has mastered middle-dealing
he is about as dangerous as a man can get
with a deck of cards in his hands.*
—John Scarne

This is one man's hard-won solution to the nagging problem of the cut. In theory, it is the ultimate solution: no need to reverse the packets, no jogs, no breaks, no bridges, no crimps. The cheat sets up his stack on the bottom of the deck, allows the cards to be legitimately cut, and then deals the setup directly from the center of the pack.

When rumor of this sleight surfaced in the 1920s, it was dismissed as a pipe dream, beyond the grasp of mortals, no way José. Today there are several versions. Here we'll consider the original breakthrough method invented by Allen "Bill" Kennedy, a midwestern farm boy and professional card sharp.

The work: Kennedy's innovation is really an extension of the bottom deal, done from the center of the pack. As the cheat completes the obligatory cut, he places the original bottom half of the pack (containing the stack) on the top half, but slightly offset to the right—creating a small overhang at the outer right corner.

The pack is now lifted from the table and transferred to the left hand for dealing. The left index finger covers the front edge of the deck, screening the overhang, the remaining fingers are at the right side of the pack, and the thumb lies across the top. Now for the difficult part.

As the right hand comes over to apparently deal the top card, the left fingers squeeze inward, severely buckling all of the cards beneath the shelf. The tip of the middle finger now presses upward against the original bottom card. As pressure on the buckled cards is relaxed, everything slides back to the right, *including the original bottom card,* which automatically pivots off the left index fin-

ger and pops out the side of
the deck (Fig. 1). This is completely shielded by the back
of the right hand (Fig. 2) as it
comes over and mimes tak-
ing the top card, but comes
away with the center card instead. The card can be dealt
facedown or faceup, depending on the situation. (If the
position in Fig. 2 seems awkward, bear in mind that *all* of

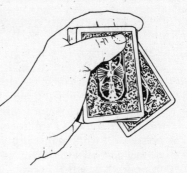

Fig. 1

the cards, including those
that come from the top, are
dealt in an identical way,
thereby achieving, in Erdnase's phrase, the "uniformity of action" required to
normalize potentially suspicious actions.) With this brief
description, and ten years of
practice, you should have it
down.

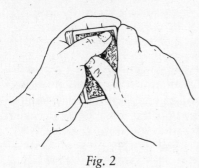

Fig. 2

Prevention and Detection

Chances of encountering the center dealer are virtually nil; the
move is insanely difficult, requiring years of practice, crushing
hand strength, delicate touch, and the appearance of complete re-
laxation. That's probably why most cheats, despite the move's
theoretical utility, have taken easier routes, such as having an ally
cut the cards. Magicians, on the other hand, are challenged by the
move and new handlings continue to evolve.

THE MAGICIAN AND THE CARDSHARP

Kennedy's masterpiece might never have seen the light of day were it not for Dai Vernon—a brilliant card artist obsessed with every facet of card artifice, no matter the source. Widely regarded as the most influential close-up magician of the twentieth century, Vernon was not yet a teenager when he discovered Erdnase and realized that the most sophisticated work with cards—sleights and principles completely unknown to magicians—was the work of cheats and sharpers. Any whiff of a rumor, any hint of something new, and Vernon was off in monomaniacal pursuit, no matter the time, place, or responsibilities of family life.

Vernon got wind of Kennedy's whereabouts by chance in 1932, when a friend took him to meet a professional card sharp named Amador Villasenor, then residing in a Wichita, Kansas, jail cell awaiting trial on a murder charge. Villasenor didn't know Kennedy's name or address, only that he lived somewhere around Kansas City, Missouri—then the nation's capital of hot jazz and illicit gambling—and that he could deal flawlessly from the center of the deck.

Two months later Vernon was standing on Kennedy's doorstep. Posing as an East Coast card mechanic who plied his trade on transatlantic steamers, Vernon talked his way into the house, and after demonstrating his own prowess with gambling sleights (pilgrims always went first), convinced Kennedy to share his remarkable method.

The Vernon-Kennedy story forms the centerpiece of Karl Johnson's *The Magician and the Cardsharp*, a richly layered account of the life and times of both men and their shared obsession with cards. Kennedy's secret remained tightly held until 1978, when it appeared in *The Magic and Methods of Ross Bertram*. Kennedy died in 1961. Vernon died in 1992, at the age of 98.

PRACTICE, PRACTICE, PRACTICE, OR HOW DO YOU GET TO CARNEGIE HALL?

Kennedy had the idea for the center deal long before he had the chops to execute it. Not knowing how to develop his finger skills, he took his problem, ingeniously, to the Kansas City Conservatory of Music. There he was given two sets of exercises utilized by concert performers. In one exercise, he was instructed to hold corks between the fingers of each hand, and then squeeze the corks and bend the fingers inward. The second exercise consisted of pressing the fingers against a tabletop or wall and holding the tension, first with each finger individually, then all in unison. These workouts, apparently, did the trick.

27

A FALSE OVERHAND
SHUFFLE—THE JOG SHUFFLE

The jog shuffle is one of the great utility sleights of card handling. Every professional cheat and card conjuror knows about it and uses it at every opportunity. It's convincing, casual, and apparently free of guile (actually, it's full of guile). Cheats use the shuffle to stack the deck, shift groups of cards from here to there, and mark the location for a cut.

In this chapter, we'll see how the shuffle is used to preserve a slug of cards—such as a stacked hand, a memorized sequence, or a location play—on the top or bottom of the pack, while the rest of the cards are genuinely shuffled.

The shuffle mimics the familiar overhand shuffle most of us learned as kids. I'll start by describing an honest shuffle, followed by the cheating version.

The Overhand Shuffle   The pack is held in the right hand between the thumb and middle fingers on the short ends, the index finger resting on top. In the first shuffle action two things happen at once: The right hand lifts the pack from the left, *as* the left thumb draws off a small group of cards from the top of the deck. The right hand continues with a series of up and down motions into the left, as the left thumb continues to draw off packets of cards. The right hand can also toss or slide small groups of cards into the left, the left thumb lifting to receive them. All of the motion is done by the right hand. The left hand's cards rest on the palm and the base of the fingers, supported by the ring and second fingers at the rear, and the index finger and pinkie at the ends (Fig. 1).

When all of the cards have been *shuffled off* into the left hand—in about five to ten shuffle actions—the right fingers tap the top of the pack, squaring the long edges, and the thumb and second fingers

square the short ends. The
shuffle is complete and can be
repeated.

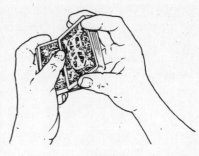

Fig. 1

The Jog Shuffle Now,
imagine the cheat has a slug
on top of the deck that goes
eight cards deep. The goal is
to shuffle in a way that appears identical to the genuine shuffle, yet not lose
control of the setup. This is
usually accomplished in the course of two shuffles: The first iso-
lates and protects the *top stock* as the rest of the cards are mixed;
the second, while also mixing cards, returns the set up to the top.
Here's how.

To begin, the left thumb draws *all of the cards in the stack* (plus
a few extras, to be sure), into the left hand as the right hand moves
up. The right hand moves slightly inward as it descends onto the
left, and the left thumb draws off a single card, positioned so that
it protrudes from the inner
end of the deck, about half
an inch (Fig. 2). This is the
jog that gives the shuffle its
name, and it bookmarks the
position of the top stock.
(When a card protrudes from
the outer end of the deck, it is
outjogged.) The right hand
now shuffles off the remainder of its cards on top of the
in-jogged card, using five to
ten shuffle actions. To sum-

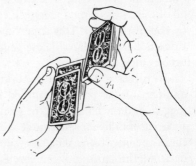

Fig. 2

marize: (1) draw off the stock, (2) in-jog one card, (3) shuffle the
rest on top. This completes the first shuffle, however, the deck is
left in an unsquared condition.

To return the stock to the top, the right hand begins a second shuffle by first squaring the deck; the extended fingers tap the top of the pack, then the short ends are squared between the thumb and fingers. In squaring the short ends, however, as the right thumb pushes the jogged card flush with the deck, it also pushes *leftward*. This causes a small gap or *break* to open on the inner end of the deck, which is held in place by the right thumb (Fig. 3). The right hand now lifts the pack from the left, maintaining the break, and begins the second shuffle by drawing off a few cards. All of the cards above the break are now shuffled off normally, using several shuffle actions, and the remaining cards—those that were below the break—are tossed as a unit onto those in the left hand. The setup is back on top.

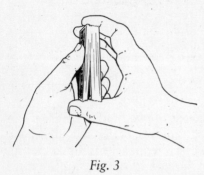

Fig. 3

The top stock can also be returned to the top without the second shuffle. The right hand concludes the first shuffle by grasping all of the cards *below* the jogged card and tossing them, as a unit, on top of the deck. This is perceived as a simple cut and the top stock is back in place. These sequences can be repeated several times.

To preserve a slug on the bottom of the deck, the top three quarters of the pack is shuffled off honestly, a single card injogged, and the balance of the pack thrown on top. As the pack is squared for the second shuffle, the cheat pulls *in* on the jogged card, opening a break *below* the original bottom portion of the deck. All the cards above the break are tossed into the left hand as a unit, and the remainder of the pack is shuffled off on top. The bottom block is back where it started.

Naturally, the cheat doesn't look at his hands during any of these shuffles. Everything is done by feel. The left thumb gauges how many cards it needs to draw off and the left pinkie stays in contact with the jogged card until the break is taken. The cards are shuffled at an even tempo. The right hand need move inward only the slightest amount to set the jog. The jog shuffle, which is also known as a *break shuffle*, is often mixed with false riffle shuffles to create a very deceptive sequence.

Prevention and Detection

Public card rooms don't allow overhand shuffling. It's not very thorough, and it's subject to abuse. Yet this shuffle is right at home in the majority of private games. It looks familiar, seems safe, and few players question it. When a cheat finds himself among players who shuffle overhand, you can be sure he'll dust if off and put it to use.

HISTORICAL NOTE

Sharpers and magicians have been in-jogging and out-jogging cards since the middle of the sixteenth century. The first English-language mention of the ruse appears in Reginald Scot's *The Discovery of Witchcraft* (1584):

You must always whilest you shuffle keepe him [the jogged card] *a little before or a little behind all the cards lieng underneath him, bestowing him, I saie, either a little beyond his fellows before, right over the forefinger,* [outjog] *or else behind the rest* [injog] *so as the little finger of the left hand may meete with it: which is the easier, the readier, and the better waie.*

The description is amazing for its attention to detail. Scot also professed to know "the lewd juggling [tricks] that chetors practice," but chose not to reveal them "lest it minister some offense to the well disposed."

Overhand shuffle cheating is difficult to spot. The tossing of unshuffled blocks can be a tell, but when the shuffle is done briskly, it is almost impossible for observers to keep track of what's happening. Easier to spot is a long run of single cards, which is almost always a sign that cards are being manipulated.

The safest procedure is to adopt casino rules: tabled riffle shuffles only. If overhand is the only way some players know how to shuffle, remember that you have the right to shuffle the deck afterward. One thorough riffle shuffle will undo most any setup.

CONTROLLING SMALL STACKS

When dealing with a small stack—five cards, for example—the cheat may choose to bypass the jog shuffle and simply *run* the cards from the top of the deck to the bottom and back, using two overhand shuffles. This is an easy and deceptive sequence.

The cheat begins by drawing off single cards until the complete stack is held by the left hand. The remaining cards are shuffled on top in a haphazard manner. The stack is now on the bottom of the pack, in reverse order. The cheat now begins a second shuffle. When the right hand's cards are nearly depleted the cheat *runs* the remaining cards into the left hand one at a time. This returns the stack to the top, in the original order. A bottom slug is controlled in a similar fashion, running it to the top and then back to the bottom.

28

UNDOING THE CUT— THE CRIMP AND THE BRIEF

One of the appealing features of the jog shuffle is how the mechanics of the shuffle lead directly into a modus operandi for overcoming the cut. The following classic methods are used by professional cheats whenever overhand shuffling is the norm.

The Crimp   Like "Forcing the Cut" (the 5th Way), the idea here is to bury the target cards in the center of the deck and have the player to the cheat's right unwittingly cut them back to the top. Instead of a bridge, the artifice is a small bend or *crimp* that is put into the inner left corner of the card. When cut into the deck, the mighty crimp maintains a separation between the cards above or below it, depending on the direction of the bend. Cutting near the crimp will cause the deck to separate *at* the crimp about eight out of ten times. Downward-crimped cards will cut to the bottom of the deck, upward-crimped cards to the top.

The work: We'll pick up the action as the cheat completes the last of his jog shuffles, exactly as described in the previous chapter. The top stock (with a secret setup on top) is drawn into the left hand, the next card in-jogged, and rest of the deck shuffled off (Fig. 1). The right fingers tap and square the top of the deck as usual; but now things change. The deck is allowed to fall flat onto the left palm so that the right hand can come over and square the pack from

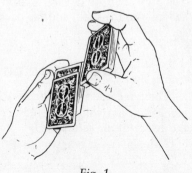

Fig. 1

above. As the right fingers and thumb push in on the short ends of the deck, the thumb also pushes *down* on the inner left corner of the in-jogged card, bending it as it enters the deck. The sides of the deck are squared and the pack is tabled in front of the cutter like a savory roast. With the crimped corner facing the cheat, the

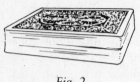

Fig. 2

gap is concealed from all angles (Fig. 2). If the gods of cheating cooperate, the unwitting accomplice will cut at the crimp, bringing the bent card to the bottom of the deck and the returning the setup to the top.

Cutting at a Brief   With an ally to his right, the cheat can use virtually the same method, *without* putting a bend in the card. All the steps are indentical to the above until the squaring of the deck. This time, the cheat squares up so that the in-jogged card continues to protrude from the rear of the pack by about one eighth of an inch (Fig. 3). This ledge, or *brief* marks the location for the cut. The cheat lifts the deck by the long sides and tables it in front of his partner.

Fig. 3

To cut at the brief the right index finger presses down on the top card, the middle finger anchors the deck from the front, and the thumb lifts *up* on the jogged card. The pressure from the index finger prevents the jogged card from sliding into the deck, and the pack is easily cut at the desired location.

Prevention and Detection

These methods are quite disarming. The cuts are made one-handed, at normal speed, and appear completely honest, even if the deck is being scrutinized.

As a player, the best way to defend against a crimp or bridge is to *consciously* cut the deck at a specific location, rather than letting the pack break open of its own accord. It's worth doing this every time you cut. If you have reason to suspect the dealer of cheating, make sure to watch the cut from start to finish, including the replacement of the deck into dealing position. If the cutter misses the crimp, the cheat still has plenty of ways to maneuver the stack back on top, such as the shift (the 51st Way) , the jump (the 1st Way), and the one-handed table hop (the 45th Way).

29

OVERHAND
SHUFFLE STACKING

There is something particularly nasty (or is it tasty?) about a cheating system that disguises its modus operandi as its opposite. Such is the nature of shuffle stacking. In the guise of mixing the cards in the interest of fairness, the cheat actually arranges them in the interest of self.

A stacked deck is one that is set to jump-start one player's hand by delivering powerhouse cards, such as trip aces, when the cards are dealt from the top of the deck. Any type of hand can be stacked, or "run up" while shuffling, and it can be arranged to fall to any position on the table. The procedure consists of culling the target cards to the top or bottom of the deck and then inserting spacer cards between them so that the stacked hand falls to the desired player. In this chapter we'll see how this is accomplished using the traditional overhand shuffle. Stacking with a riffle shuffle is the subject of the 46th Way.

The work: This material is much easier to follow with deck in hand, so play along. We'll begin with three aces on the bottom of the deck and stack them to fall to the dealer in a heads-up game.

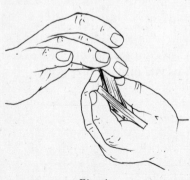

Begin by shuffling off about a quarter of the deck into the left hand. In the next shuffle action only two cards are taken into the left hand; one comes from the *top* of the deck and the other is taken from the *bottom* by the left fingers (Fig. 1). This is called a *milk shuffle* or *milk build shuffle* and is one of the basic actions of over-

Fig. 1

hand stacking. The two cards are taken simultaneously and fall onto the left hand's cards. These are an "x" card from the top of the deck with an ace beneath it.

Do two more milk shuffles, to position the remaining aces. In-jog the next card to act as a bookmark (see the 27th Way, "The Jog Shuffle") and shuffle the remaining cards on top. Cut all the cards beneath the in-jog to the top and square up. From the top down the deck should read x-A-x-A-x-A, the dealer gets the aces. Note that this stack is set up in *one* shuffle.

Things get more complex with more players in the game as additional spacer cards must be added after each milk shuffle. The number of cards depends on the number of players, but the formula is always the same: Run cards equal to the number of players, less two. There's no need to remember this if you substitute a simple counting procedure: With every milk shuffle silently count "two," and continue counting as you run cards singly into the left hand, ending when you reach the number equal to the number of players in the game. An example will make this clear. To stack three aces in a seven-handed game, put the aces on the bottom the deck and proceed as follows:

1. Shuffle off a quarter of the deck into the left hand.
2. Milk shuffle once and silently count "two."
3. Run five cards singly, silently counting "three, four, five, six, seven."
4. Milk shuffle the second ace into position, counting "two," and run five more cards, counting to seven.
5. Repeat with the third ace.
6. In-jog one card, shuffle the remaining cards on top, and cut everything below the jogged card to the top. Deal seven hands and take your bow as you turn up three aces.

In theory, the cheat can run up a straight, flush, or boat. As a practical matter, however, the setup requires way too much shuffling, because you would now have to cycle through the steps five times instead of three. Most stackers are quite happy starting off with three of a kind.

Overhand stacking has legions of variations, each with its own procedures and formulas. Hands can be stacked from the top of the deck rather than the bottom, using a combination of in-jogs and out-jogs (see *The Expert at the Card Table*). Two hands can be run up at once and the winning hand set to fall to any position at the table. Finally, the whole procedure can be folded into a series of false shuffles, cuts, and strips that cancel out any idea of a setup.

Prevention and Detection

There's a ton of procedure in overhand shuffle stacking that makes it difficult to do well. The hardest part is maintaining a natural rhythm while shifting back and forth between milk shuffles and single-card runs. Watch the dealer for changes in tempo and little stutters and hesitations that shouldn't be there. The running of single cards is also a major tell.

So is excessive speed. Stacking a hand in a seven-player game is a tedious procedure with repetitious and time-consuming steps. Even experts tend to race through the moves, lest the other players begin stomping their feet and shouting "Deal already!" On the other hand, in an easygoing, friendly, kibitzing game often nobody cares how long the shuffle takes. That's not what the night is about. Except maybe for the cheat.

You can also do what the casinos do and stick to the tabled riffle shuffle. No overhand shuffling, no overhand stacking.

STACKING THE DECK FOR HOLD 'EM

It's a good thing overhand shuffling is off-limits in public card rooms and private clubs. Otherwise a crooked dealer could feed his buddies winning hands all night long.

The following formula will set the deck to deliver pocket aces to any position at the table, any number of players. Start with the aces on the bottom of the deck and use the counting formula explained in this chapter.

1. Milk shuffle, counting "two," and continue counting and running cards until the reaching the number of players in the game.
2. Milk shuffle, counting "two," and continue counting and running cards until reaching the number of seat position where the aces are to fall.
3. In-jog one card and shuffle off the rest of the deck.
4. Cut everything below the in-jog to the top.
5. Deal and the aces will fall to the designated seat.

To inject even more juice into the stack, a kicker ace can be added to appear on the flop. Begin with three aces on the bottom of the deck.

1. Milk shuffle, counting "two," and run cards equal to the number of players.
2. Repeat step one.
3. Milk shuffle, counting "two," and run cards equal to the seat position where the aces are to fall.
4. In-jog one card and shuffle off.
5. Cut everything below the in-jog to the top.

Deal and the aces will fall to the desired position. Burn one card and deal the flop, revealing the ace.

30

HOLDING OUT

My friend, if the king of spades is not under your hand, I owe you an apology.
—Anonymous gambler of the Old West,
after nailing his opponent's hand to the
card table with a bowie knife

Holding out is the art of playing poker with more cards than your opponent has. The cheat gets extra cards by removing them from the deck secretly during play; then he switches them in and out to improve his hand.

Trust me when I tell you that this is a huge subject. Cheats and tricksters have devoted billions of brain cells to figuring out how to steal, conceal, and switch cards without being caught. The ingenious mechanical solutions are the subject of the next chapter. Here we take the purist approach—doing it with nothing but your god-given hands. The drama has four acts: steal, conceal, switch, and clean up.

The Steal   The cheat can steal the initial card virtually anytime he gets his hands on the pasteboards. He can palm from the deck, cop from the discards, or pilfer from his own hand on another player's deal. Exactly how he does this depends on the game. In draw, the cheat might use a *classic palm*. After squeezing open the hand for a peek, the cheat shifts the target card to the door position (at the face of the packet), closes the fan, and briefly rests the cards on the left fingers. This is a momentary "rest position" in which the cheat apparently is thinking about whether to play the hand. However, under cover of the right hand, which holds the cards from above, the bottom card is slid into the right palm (Fig. 1, seen from below). The hands turn inward and the cards are respread (Fig. 2). When it's the cheat's turn to act, he folds and tosses four cards into the muck as five. He's now one ahead.

Copping the initial card in seven-card stud is trickier because the cheat must steal a hole card. Top technicians do this with spectacular ease, appearing merely to peek at their cards as they pivot the innermost card into the palm, sometimes with one hand. A less difficult approach is to thumb-shuttle the innermost card into the palm of choice, as both hands lift the pocket

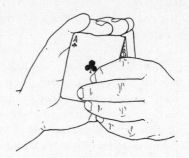

Fig. 1

Fig. 2

cards for a peek (Fig. 3). The single hole card is then returned to the table, covered by the up-card. The palming hand rests on the table, the card clipped between the thumb and the pinkie. This is called the *gambler's flat palm*. Eventually the hand is mucked, except for the palmed card.

Impossible to holdout in hold 'em? Duh . . . where'd the other card go? Actually, not a problem. When the cheat has a card he wants, he signals his partners. They fold ahead of him, starting a discard pile. Then the cheat folds, palming one card and mucking the other as if it was two. This is rare, but clearly doable.

Over the course of several hands, the cheat can cop and hold on to two or three cards. While some hustlers do this, it is considered

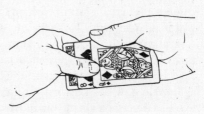

Fig. 3

dangerous. Experienced players can spot a short deck and call for a count. Most professionals steal only a single card, usually a picture.

Hiding the Card   Now that he's got the card, what does he do with it? Some sharpers keep right on playing, dangling the "dirty" hand over the edge of the table, or using it to hold cards (Fig. 2), pick up a drink, or toss in chips. This type of cheat is looking for a quick score, hoping to use the copped card on the very next hand and turn it into a winner. Most holdout artists, however, quickly "go south," squirreling the card away until it can be used to inflict maximum damage later on. Al Smith does the math in *Poker to Win*: "Two or three big hands held against other big hands are worth twenty big hands that have no opposition."

So where does the cheat stash the card while in lurk mode? Stealer's choice. In cowboy days, the most popular hideouts were inside a ruffled shirt or frilly cuffs, behind the vest and inside the boots. A centuries-old concealment, still used today, is under the thigh or behind the knee (the cheat pretends to be adjusting his chair as he ditches or retrieves the card). Some cheats dump and retrieve from their pockets, a ploy that works well as long as the cheat *justifies* the action of dipping into his pocket by bringing something out or putting something away (a lighter, Tic Tacs, a pack of gum). An unexpected concealment is under the shirt collar at the back of the neck. The cheat must be seated against the wall for this one; the hand with the palmed card slides around the side of the neck and, under cover of a massaging action, deposits the card.

The Exchange   Eventually, the requirements of the scam converge: There's a raft of cash on the table and the held-out card will make the hand. How do you get it back in play? In any of several ways. In draw, for example, the cheat might place his cards on the table directly in front of him, repalm the copped card, and then add it to the tabled cards as he picks them up again. He now has six cards in the hand and must palm out the extra as described above. Or, more crudely, he can bring his cards to the edge of the table and drop the unwanted card into his lap.

In stud or hold 'em, the palmed card can be slid *under* the hole cards as they are lifted for the peek (Fig. 4) and the top card is eventually palmed out. Or the palmed card can be added to the top of the hole cards and the innermost card palmed out as described earlier. A hole card can also be switched *in the act of turning it over.* A classic method used in five-card

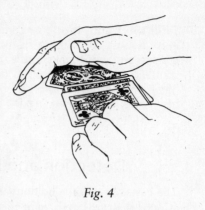

Fig. 4

stud is to sweep the hole card into the lap while pretending to turn it face up, revealing the palmed card in its place. Hole-card switches are among the most difficult of all gambling sleights and the most amazing to watch when demonstrated by an expert.

The Cleanup   After the laydown the cheat will still have an extra card. Some cheats hold on to it for the next game, but the safest course is to clean up immediately after the showdown, lest anyone suspect the deck is short and call for a countdown. The standard method is to simply toss the extra card into the discards, along with the rest of the hand. If the discards are too far away, the cheat will keep the card and add it to the pack on his own deal.

CASINO SCAMS

Holding out in a casino or public card room is rare because of how often the cards are counted. But the system is not foolproof. A cheat may wait until the dealer counts the cards, and then palm one on the next deal and try to use it quickly. Collusion is also a possibility. A crooked dealer can simply *pretend* to count a full deck while his partner holds out. In one scam, the cheats *started* the game with the cards already held out: The dealer's new deck was three cards short, and his partner came to the table with the set in his pocket. All of these scams, however, are rapidly becoming antiques thanks to the growing use of automated shuffling machines. These devices not only speed up the game and ensure a thorough shuffle, they also count the cards after every game, making holding out impossible.

Detection and Prevention

The best way to foil a holdout artist is to do what the casinos do. Count the cards and count them often. Change decks from time to time, alternating decks with different color backs.

If you want to *catch* the cheat rather than merely thwart him, focus on the suspect's hands. Are they always in view, or does one traffic above and below the table? Palming cards gracefully and invisibly is not easy, and unless done perfectly, there are tells. Look out for a stiff hand with the fingers held rigidly together, or a hand that stays flat on the table and never moves. There are also certain postures that can tip off an expert, such as resting a hand on the opposite forearm, or dangling the wrist over the edge of the table, the back of the hand out of sight. Both can indicate a palmed card. Also, suspect the player who—when a short deck is counted—stands up, looks around, and discovers the missing card under the table. It likely came from under his thigh.

THE ELUSIVE TRICKSTER— SLIPPING OUT OF TROUBLE

What does a holdout artist do when about to be caught red-handed? George Joseph, one of the world's top cheating-detection experts, recounts the following solution from his youth:

One time in a poker game I was holding out a pair of kings. Well, somebody at the game decided to count down the deck. Of course, they counted 50 cards instead of 52. Great concern fell over the table at this point. If I waited long enough, they would of course get to me. I needed to take control of the situation, as bad as it was. As soon as the guy who counted the cards placed them on the table, I grabbed the deck, added the two kings back on top, and said, "Let me count those cards." The question is, How many cards did I count? Most people say, Of course, you counted 52. Wrong. Hello! If I counted 52 cards, the entire table would know that I had added the missing cards to the deck. I finished counting the cards, and even though there were now 52 cards, I slammed the deck down on the table and yelled, "Fifty cards! You rotten bastards!"

By this time, the guys running the game had come to the table to see what the trouble was. Well, the next poor bastard who picked up the deck counted, you guessed it, 52 cards. He took all the heat. I tried to put the guys running the game on the defensive and cover myself by changing the order of the count. I said, "What the f— is going on here? I counted 50 cards, this guy counted 50 cards, and now all of a sudden there's 52." I made it sound like I counted first. "I can't fade this b———, I'm getting out of here!" Sometimes I wonder if the poor guy who picked up the cards after me realized it was me who added the pair of kings. Sometimes I wonder, but not very often.

This story, slightly abbreviated, comes from Joseph's entertaining *The 101 Most Asked Questions about Las Vegas and Casino Gambling.*

31

HOLDING OUT—
THE GADGETS

*Dear Sir: In reply to yours, there is only one sure way
to win at cards, etc., and that is to get Tools to work
with and then to use them with discretion, which is
the secret of all Gambling and the way that all
Gamblers make their money.*
—Cover letter from a turn-of-the-century
gambling supply house

By the 1860s, cheating entrepreneurs were peddling a full line
of "advantage tools" aimed at the wannabe holdout man.
These consisted mainly of passive holding devices known as *bugs*,
mechanical card-delivery systems known as *machines,* and gimmicked holdout tables known as *furniture*. While much of this apparatus was obsolete by the 1920s (and a lot of it was useless to
begin with), the practical devices survive in modern form.

Bugs   A bug is a portable hiding place that attaches to the
underside of the table and is used to stash held-out cards. The English stage magician John Nevil Maskelyne described the proto-
type in *Sharps and Flats* (1894). "The bug is simply a straight
piece of watchspring, bent at one end. The end nearest the bend is
inserted into the handle of a very small shoemaker's awl" (Fig. 1).
The point of the awl is pressed into the bottom of the table directly in front of the cheat, with the spring projecting just beyond
the table's edge. To work the device the cheat "stands the cards on

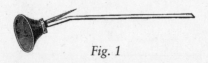

Fig. 1

edge upon the table, with their faces towards him, holding them with both hands. The card or cards which he wishes to hold out are then brought in front of the others, and with the thumbs they are quietly slid under the table between it and the spring."

This is really a brilliant way to switch and ditch cards. It's simple, portable, easy to use, and allows the cheat to keep his hands above the table at all times. Modern descendents of the device work the same way. The card cheat Walter Irving Scott used a bug of his own design made from a coiled watch spring attached to a penny with a spike soldered to it. James Swain, in his novel *Deadman's Bluff,* describes a bug made from large paper clip jammed into a wad of Silly Putty.

The Bean Shooter   This simple device enables the cheat to hide cards inside the lining of his coat sleeve. It's about as low-tech as you can get, consisting of a plastic card clip attached to a few rubber bands tied together. One end of the bands is pinned inside the lining of the jacket near the elbow, and the other end is stretched to the edge of the sleeve. The clip has a small hook at the end that is slipped over the rim of the sleeve, keeping the device just out of sight. To hold out, the cheat uses the opposite hand to draw the clip out of the sleeve and into the palm. The card is fed into the clip and the unit is allowed to retract until the card is needed.

The Short Sleeve Holdout   The gimmick is simply a small, round, or wedge-shaped piece of cardboard or plastic attached to a heavy elastic band. The unit is worn high on the upper arm, under a loose-fitting, short-sleeve shirt. The cheat palms the card in the opposite hand and slides it in and out of the clip as he apparently massages his arm.

Mechanical Holdouts   This class of devices includes an ingenious assortment of mostly historical gizmos designed to shuttle cards from their hiding places—up the sleeve, inside the jacket, behind the vest—into and out of the cheat's waiting palm. The earliest models appeared shortly after the Civil War and were promoted as an alternative to difficult sleight of hand. By pressing a concealed lever, a "lazy tongs" apparatus would extend from within the coat sleeve and deliver a clip—endearingly known as a *cheat*, *sneak*, or *thief*—into the palm. By relaxing pressure, the device would retract, taking the held-out card with it (Fig. 2).

Despite the promise of easy operation most "machines" were

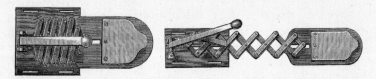

Fig. 2

awkward and unreliable. Until P. J. "The Lucky Dutchman" Kepplinger came along. A San Francisco card hustler and mechanical wizard, Kepplinger designed and built the ne plus ultra of holdout machines. Not only was it reliable, it could be operated with no visual motion. Kepplinger could palm a card and it would vanish from his hand in an instant, or he could flash an empty hand, turn his palm down, and the card would be back—without *any* tells whatsoever.

The secret to the invisible operation was that the motive force took place out of sight, under the table. The unit, strapped on under the clothes, consisted of a complex arrangement of cables and pulleys that ran between the knees, up the thigh to the hip, from there to the shoulder, then down the arm, terminating in a metal slide concealed inside a pair of metal jaws hidden inside a double shirt sleeve (Fig. 3). Upon sitting down at the table, Kepplinger would reach through a slit in his trousers and string the cable between his knees. When he spread his knees apart, the jaws opened, the rod moved down the sleeve, and the *sneak* extended into the palm, clipping the palmed card. Closing the knees reversed the process.

Kepplinger never intended to share his invention with his fellow sharps, since he used it to outcheat them week after week. But eventually, the chumps wised up. (How was it that the Lucky Dutchman *never* lost?) One night, three of his poker pals pinned

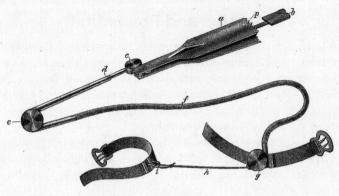

Fig. 3

Kepplinger to his chair, stripped off his jacket, and discovered the promised land. However, instead of "lumping" their erstwhile buddy, they persuaded Kepplinger to build three more units. That was in 1888. A couple of years later, the gaff supply houses were selling their own versions of the "knee spread" or "San Francisco" holdout. The catalogue price was $100, or about $2,000 in today's dollars.

Holdout Tables   Gaffed poker tables come from the same era as holdout machines. Designed to look like conventional poker tables, the crooked versions concealed a network of springs and levers that would open a sliding panel on the tabletop— hidden behind the cheat's hand—when activated by knee pressure from below. The tables were marketed to gambling houses and wealthy individuals who didn't like to lose.

Although rare, modern versions do exist. In *Gambling Scams*, Darwin Ortiz describes a souped-up table available in the 1980s that was built to deliver held-out cards to any position at the table, via a lazy Susan–type mechanism. The typical clientele were "invariably affluent, respected members of their community who regularly played cards with their friends for stakes which made the two-thousand-dollar investment and the practice time worthwhile."

Detection and Prevention

It takes nerves of steel and a touch of insanity to sit down at a card table trussed up in a Kepplinger-style holdout machine. Although we get a quick peek at the device in the movie *Shade*—it's tucked in "The Dean's" (Sylvester Stallone) briefcase—it is highly unlikely that you or I will ever be trimmed by a "machine man." Wearing the device is simply too risky.

Bugs, bean shooters, and sleeve holdouts remain a staple of the cheater's trade. Stay alert for key tells, such as bringing the cards to the edge of the table, shielded by the back of the hands, or repetitive massaging of the upper arm. One instance means nothing. Again and again is suspicious. If you suspect a bug, drop something under the table and have a look. To watch a holdout table in action, check out Sal Piacente's entertaining DVD *Poker Cheats Exposed*.

The best defense against holding out is to count the cards. Even if the count is correct, count them again later. If there is a holdout man at the table, you can be sure he'll think twice about moving.

TRUTH IN ADVERTISING

Advertising copy for The Bug, from the catalogue of E. N. Grandin, a New York City cheating-supply house that operated during the Civil War era:

> *This is an entirely new invention, for the purpose of "holding out" any number of cards. . . . It can be carried in the vest pocket all the time, is always ready for use, and not liable to get out of order, but should it do so any watchmaker can put it in order for a trifle, as the whole expense of manufacture is only about fifty cents. "Then why ask $3.00 for it?" you may say. For this reason—That one is all you will ever want to buy, as they do not wear out like cards. Also, after seeing it*

you can get one made as well as I can, and make them for your friends and sell them to all the sporting men in your vicinity, thereby injuring my trade and I get nothing for my invention; and you will wonder that the thing was never thought of before. With it you can "hold out" one or twenty cards, shift and make up your hand to suit, and your hands and person are at perfect liberty all the time. Your opponent may look in your lap and up your sleeve, but there is nothing to be seen! After having used it once you would not be without it for any price.

32

A QUICK AND EASY STACK

This is a quick and effective system for kick-starting any draw or stud poker hand with three of a kind. Unlike some of the stacking methods explained elsewhere, this setup is in place before the cheat even touches the cards. That's because the stack is engineered by the cheat's partner, seated to his right, during *his* deal. Although the method involves a breach in poker etiquette— the scammer must briefly look at the faces of the discards—this indiscretion occurs at just the right moment and appears perfectly innocent to the uninformed. By the time the deck reaches the cheat it is, so to speak, a done deal.

The work: The first order of business is to locate a set. After dealing the last card of his deal, the cheat's partner—who has dropped out early to get a head start—combines the undealt cards with the discards, briefly looks through them, and culls the target cards to the top (see the 6th Way). If he can't easily locate trips, he substitutes other strong starter cards, such as a high pair with a kicker. Often these can be found together and brought to the top with a single cut.

Now the actual stacking procedure begins. The method is low-tech and consists of peeling cards from one hand to the other, putting them back where they came from, and repeating the process. To the other players, this activity must appear to be an idle toying with the cards, or a nervous habit, or a preliminary shuffle, or an obsessive-compulsive disorder, anything other that what it actually is—a counting procedure.

Say it's a five-handed game. To follow along, put three aces on top of fifteen or twenty cards (these represent combined discards and talon). Hold the packet in the right hand between the thumb on the inner short end, the fingers on the outer. With the left thumb, peel 11 cards one at a time onto the left palm and fingers (Fig. 1). Replace this packet on the right hand's cards and repeat, this time counting and replacing 10 cards. Repeat this action twice more, counting and replacing 6 and 5 cards respectively. The stack is now set, with the aces in first, sixth and eleventh positions, ready

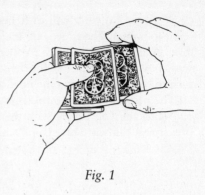

Fig. 1

to fall to the one-seat in a five-handed game. The identical results can be achieved by running single cards using an overhand shuffle, but the appearance is not as casual.

Following the showdown, the new dealer assembles the pack with the setup on top. He then false-shuffles and, if necessary, adds a few random cards to the top of the stack so that the aces will fall to his partner. In this example, the partner is in the four-seat, so the cheat adds three cards to the stack.

Now let's briefly return to the counting procedure. The formula, of course, depends on the number of players in the game. In this five-handed example, the count was 11-10-6-5. For a six-handed game the count is 13-12-7-6; for four players it's 9-8-5-4. One way to remember this is by working backward: The last number of the formula is always equal to the number of players in the game; the third number adds one; the second number is double the number of players, and the first number adds one.

Prevention and Detection

There is a glaring tell to this type of stacking that makes it obvious to anyone in the know—the running of long strings of cards, one at a time, from hand to hand. Spot this and you spot trouble.

On the other hand, the whole thing can breeze right by. Because the player toying with the cards is not in the game and because all the cards have already been dealt, the tinkering doesn't seem to matter. The procedure may appear lengthy, but it can be done briskly, and the cheat's partner (the upcoming dealer) can always buy some extra time for the stacker by stalling when it's his turn to bet or call during the final round.

The best way to avoid this ruse is to stop it before it starts by enforcing the "no toying with the discards" rule. This ounce of prevention can ward off an epidemic of miseries.

33

CHEATING WITH THE CUT CARD

A cut card is a thin, opaque, card-sized piece of plastic used by public card rooms as a safeguard against flashing, peeking, and bottom dealing. The shuffled deck is cut directly onto the cut card and the cut completed. The cut card remains on the bottom of the pack throughout the game. But that won't stop a determined cheat who can flash, peek, and bottom deal anyway, as we'll see below. But here's the kicker: The cheat's fevered brain has also figured out how to transform the cut card from a guardian of the gates into a multifarious cheating tool with diabolical applications, such as tracking a slug or engineering a superlative false cut.

Peeking and Flashing   A simple enabler to the basic flash is to use a bridge-size cut card with a poker-size deck. The difference in width is three sixteenths of an inch, which is just enough to expose the index of the bottom card when the cut card is flush left to the deck. (See the 10th Way, "Flashing.") If a house dealer is the only one to handle the cut card, the size discrepancy will likely go unnoticed by the players. A poker-size cut card can also be trimmed for the same purpose.

For peeking, the cheat simply slides the cut card slightly to the right with the left fingers, as the right hand holds the deck from above. The back of the right hand screens the deck from the right side and the projecting cut card isn't seen. The left hand provides shade by tossing in chips, as the right tilts forward, exposing the bottom card to a downward glance. When the deck is transferred to the left hand, the cut card is pulled flush. The cheat can also use the rotation peek in conjunction with a *translucent* cut card (see "Bottom Card Peek," the 9th Way). If the cut card is thin enough, the bottom card bleeds through.

Bottom Dealing   All the subway dealer needs is access to the bottom card. One approach is to pull down the inner right corner of the cut card with the left pinkie, giving the right fingers access. If the cut card is flexible, as many are, it can be buckled by the left fingers, again providing access. Dealing the second card from the bottom is known as a *Greek deal* and was invented so that cellar dealers could "prove" they weren't dealing from the bottom by flashing the same bottom card from time to time.

Another approach is to palm the bottom three or four cards in the left hand before the cut, and replace them *under* the cut card. The *gambler's cop* is a favorite move. As the cheat squares the long sides of the deck by sliding it inward and out between the left thumb and fingers, the bottom cards are clipped between the base of the thumb and fingers. The right hand tables the deck and begins the cut to the cut card, as the left hand tilts inward or rotates palm-down, hiding the copped cards (Fig. 1). The cut is completed and the deck is returned to the left hand, which turns palm-up at the last moment, adding the copped cards to the bottom.

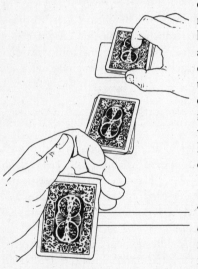

Fig. 1

Positioning a Slug   This is pretty sinister. As the cheat clears the table following the showdown, his partner tosses over a set of culled cards to be stacked for the upcoming deal. Instead of maneuvering them to the top or bottom of the deck, the cheat marks their location by dropping the undealt cards from the previous game—the cut card beneath them—directly on top of the setup! This is very casual and disarming. The rest of the cards are assembled in any order and added to the deck. The cheat squares the pack, thumbs through it, and removes the cut card in order to shuffle. At the same time, he cuts all of the cards *below* the cut card to the top of the deck. The stack is now in place and ready for further manipulation. (For another application, see "Stacking the Flop in Hold 'Em," the 43rd Way.)

A Devious Cut-Card False Cut   This is a highly deceptive false cut that mimics a familiar casino-approved cut. The dealer invites a player to insert the cut card halfway into the pack at any spot. The cut card and all the cards above it are cut to the table, and the cut completed. This is the real deal, a genuine cut. To simulate the same, but *not* cut the deck, the cheat sets up the sequence by shifting the bottom third of the deck to the top, and holding a

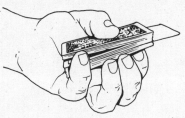

break between the sections with the left pinkie. The deck is extended to the cheat's partner who inserts the cut card anywhere in the lower two thirds of the deck (Fig. 2). The cheat now slides forward all

Fig. 2

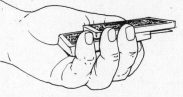

of the cards above the break until they are flush with the out-jogged cut card (Fig. 3). The players mistakenly assume this to be *all* of the cards above the cut card. The right hand

Fig. 3

cuts all of the out-jogged cards and the cut card to the table as a unit. That leaves the left hand holding the original top of the deck, which is added to the tabled cards to complete the alleged cut. If you haven't run through this with deck in hand, the experience is enlightening.

Prevention and Detection

Despite these vulnerabilities, the use of a cut card can and does prevent many types of cheating as well as inadvertent flashing. Make sure the card is opaque and the same size as the deck. A rigid cut card provides the best protection against the bottom deal, although chances of running up against a cheat who can do a Greek deal with a cut card are slim to none.

The most devious use of the cut card is as a tracking device. There's no reason to leave it in the middle of the deck as the cards are corralled for the next deal. Watch out for this. Also, use the cut card in the standard, casino-approved way. The tabled deck should be cut directly onto the cut card, and the cut completed, using one hand.

34

STRIPPERS

The benefit of these cards can be estimated only in one way, and that is: How much money has your opponent got?
—E. M. Grandin gambling supply catalogue

How's this for a demonstration of card mastery? The cheat, or magician (or you, gentle reader), is blindfolded; can't see a thing. Anyone shuffles the deck and hands it to the sightless dealer. He shuffles once or twice, cuts, snaps his fingers for juju, and deals the four aces from the top of the deck. Just like that.

The secret is an old one, going back to at least 1749, when it was exposed by mathematician and magic dealer Edme-Gilles Guyot. The aces—or any valuable cards the cheat desires—are *wider* than the other cards. No matter where they're situated in the deck, they can be located by feel alone and instantly *stripped out* by running the thumb and fingers down the long sides of the pack. The cards pop out like magic and can immediately be placed on the top or bottom of the deck for further manipulation.

You can buy a stripper deck from a magic shop for under ten bucks. However, these are *not* the kind of strippers used by card cheats. Magic shop strippers are wedge shaped. The entire deck is trimmed so that the cards taper slightly from one end to the other. When any card is rotated 180 degrees, the wider end protrudes from the narrow end of the deck and the card is easily stripped. The problem with this as a cheating tool is that after a few hands, many random cards will be turned end for end, due to the way players shuffle and muck their hands. At that point, there's no predicting which cards will be stripped out.

Cheats solved this problem by inventing belly strippers. In this ingenious system, the target cards are convex. Rather than tapering, both ends are equal in width but the cards bulge from the middle. No proper orientation is required.

Since you can't actually widen cards (spilling beer on them only makes them thicker), belly strippers are made by narrowing all the cards *except* the target cards. Professional cheats use a card trimmer, a device made specifically for this purpose, and sold by cheating-supply houses, past and present (Fig. 1). About one thirty-second of an inch is trimmed from each long side. The corners are then re-

Fig. 1

rounded using a custom-machined tool known as a corner-rounder. Finally, the target cards are trimmed into belly shape and returned to the deck. Serious cheats then rebox and reseal the deck to restore a pristine appearance.

The same kind of work can be applied to the ends of the deck, rather than the long sides, creating *end strippers*. The key cards are longer than the others and are stripped out as the deck is shuffled overhand.

Strippers are mainly used to cull desired cards from a shuffled deck and bring them to the top or bottom. Some cheats work with only a few strippers, such as three aces, securing them several times during the course of an evening. Other scams involve multiple key cards. In one ancient dodge reported by Gerritt M. Evans (*How Gamblers Win*), the key cards are ten cards of the same suit, including the ace; in other words, two flushes. When the time is right, the cheat strips all ten cards to the top of the deck and gives the pack one pure riffle shuffle, which inserts a spacer card between each of the stripper cards. The deck is now set to deal two flushes in a four-handed game of draw; one goes to the sucker, the other to the cheat's partner (or the cheat himself). Because the deck has been legitimately shuffled, there's no telling which player will receive which cards. If the cheat's partner gets the ace, he knows he has the winning hand and plays the sucker for all he's worth. If not, he drops out. In a heads-up game, the cheat forgets about inserting the spacer cards and just deals.

Frank Garcia describes a similar ruse in which the key cards are A-A-A, K-K-K, 5-5-5-5. Dealt to two players in any combination, these cards can deliver an assortment of high hands: two pair, three of a kind, a full house, and four of a kind. By analyzing his own hand, the cheat deduces whether he has the winner and plays accordingly. For example:

Cheat has: A-A-5-5-K	Opponent must have K-K-5-5-A	Cheat wins
Cheat has: 5-5-5-K-K	Opponent must have A-A-A-K-5	Cheat wins
Cheat has: K-K-K-A-5	Opponent must have 5-5-5-A-A	Cheat loses
Cheat has: A-A-A-K-K	Opponent must have 5-5-5-5-K	Cheat loses

The possibilities become dizzying when belly strippers are combined with end strippers *in the same deck*. This gives the cheat two entirely different sets of cards which he can call upon, both individually and in combination.

One final example. The key cards consist of a virtually unbeatable hand (2-3-4-5-6 of spades, for example) which the cheat will use one time and one time only. What's ingenious about this scam is that the cheat can deal himself this hand as often as he wishes, yet never play it or show the cards unless the pot is right. If there's no action, the cheat drops out, plays honestly for a while, and tries again later.

Prevention and Detection

Fortunately, strippers are easy to detect if you know what you're looking for. To check for belly strippers, hold the deck firmly at one end, between the right thumb and middle finger. Now draw the left thumb and middle fingers, on opposite sides of the pack, along the entire length of the cards. Turn the deck 180 degrees and repeat. If strippers are present, they'll slide right out. Repeat the same test on the short end of the deck to check for end strippers.

IN-STRIPPERS

An in-stripper is the opposite of a belly stripper and works in a different way. Rather than bellying out, the card is trimmed in the center to give it a subtle hourglass shape. Owing to the slight notch created by the hourglass, if the thumb and fingers cut the deck at the approximate location of the indentation, all the cards *above* the stripper will be cut off. When the cut is completed, the stripper will be on top of the deck.

This has several applications. For example, by in-stripping the aces there's an excellent chance that the cutter will unknowingly cut one to the top of the deck as he cuts for the deal. If the cheat has a partner in the one-seat, he's off to a great start.

The in-stripping also allows the cheat to cull the aces to the top of the deck with a series of cuts and riffle shuffles. On the first shuffle, the cheat cuts at an in-stripper and shuffles so that the ace falls last. The process is then repeated: The cheat cuts at a second ace and shuffles it on top of the first. Depending on where they lie in the deck, two, three, or all four aces can be brought to the top and stacked to fall to any position at the table (see the 46th Way, "Riffle Stacking").

Finally, a single in-stripper can be used to mark the location for the cut. For example, suppose a bottom dealer has culled a hand to the basement. He cuts at the in-stripper and riffle shuffles so as to keep the slug on the bottom and bring the in-stripper to the top. After additional false shuffles, the cheat cuts the bottom quarter of the deck to the top—placing it directly on top of the in-stripper—followed by another quarter of the deck. The cheat's partner now cuts at the in-stripper and the slug is back on the bottom.

35

SURVEILLANCE

There are cozeners abroad; therefore
it behooves men to be wary . . .
—Shakespeare, *The Winter's Tale*

Here's another medley of methods by which cheats win the information wars. No sleight of hand, no memorization, no marked cards, no partner at the table, completely legitimate shuffles, cuts and deals—yet the cheat knows all.

The secret is espionage. Somewhere close at hand, or in the next room, or down the block, a secret agent is peeking over the sucker's shoulder, reading his cards, and signaling, whispering, or Instant Messaging a report to the cheat.

Kibitzers and Other Observers   Not-so-innocent bystanders have been part of cheating scams since about five minutes after cards were invented. "You can scarcely avoid folly if they are against you," Cardano warned some five centuries ago. "They [the onlookers] will indicate to your opponent by foot or by hand that the decision he has made is not the right one." Nor should you trust those who view your cards and make side bets in your favor, Reginald Scot cautioned 1584, "for whilest they look in your game without suspicion [i.e., innocently], they discover it [reveal it] by signs to your adversaries with whome they bet, yet are their confederates."

Cheating literature is rich in such schemes. Gilbert Walker, writing in 1520, described a setup in which the spy was a seamstress. Seated behind one of the players, she would look at his cards and "by the shift or slow drawing of her needle give a token to the cheater what was the cozen's [sucker's] game."

When riverboat crews worked the scheme, they boarded ship at different stops to avoid the appearance of knowing each other. One hustler joined the game while the other, known as an "itimer," stood behind the victim and relayed information. Signals were simple—all that was being signaled was the strength of a hand, not particular cards—yet clever. "One gambler," wrote a historian of the period, "favored a walking stick, which he held at various angles; another who pretended to be an affable half-wit, wandered through the saloon sawing out coded snatches of music on the violin." Yet another chewed on a cigar and sent smoke signals.

The Peek Store   Now let's take our spy out of the card room and move him next door where he can observe the game through a hole in the wall. This approach, which goes back to the days of the pharaohs, is known in scamdom as a *peek store* (the term also refers to any crooked gambling joint or rigged carnival game). The scammer drills a hole in the wall where he can literally look over the sucker's shoulder, zero in on his cards, and signal his partner via mechanical or electronic means.

Peek stores were a regular, if hidden, feature in the thousands of "steer joints" and cheateries that peppered the American landscape before legalized gambling. Spy holes were built into the back rooms of pool halls, restaurants, social clubs—anywhere gamblers might congregate. George Joseph describes a peek store built into a kitchen cabinet, for those "friendly" home games.

Novelist James Swain, whose fictional sleuth Tony Valentine specializes in catching cheats, tipped a clever camouflage for a peek store set up in the back room of a bar or pool hall. The gimmick is a Plexiglas beer sign that is more heavily tinted on one side than the other. This gives the sign a natural one-way property; it is transparent from the back, opaque from the front. The sign is mounted over the peep hole, obscuring it, and the sucker is seated with his back to the sign.

A classic version of the scam was described by George Devol, the greatest of the riverboat cheats, in his *Forty Years a Gambler on the Mississippi*. Devol set up shop on a retired steamer in Baton Rouge, Louisiana, that had been converted into a hotel frequented by gamblers. He and his partners rented the stateroom adjacent to the card room and drilled a hole through the bulkhead. "We had a good boy that liked to lie down and make money, so we would put him in the upper berth while the game was in progress. He would look through the peep-hole, and if our friend had one pair he would pull the wire once; if two pair, twice; if threes, three times; if fours, four times, etc." The wire ran under the floor between the two rooms and, when tugged, caused a nail to emerge through a hole under the card table. Devol kicked off his boots, placed his foot over the hole, and raked in the money.

Long-Distance Spying   Now let's evict our spy from the building and send him (or, in this case, her) down the street to scope out the sucker's hand through a pair of high-powered binoculars and report back via wireless transmitter. If the scenario sounds familiar, it may be because you saw the scene in the film *Goldfinger*. The inspiration for that fiction, according to Jonathan Van Meter's *The Last Good Time*, was a real swindle run out of Miami's Fontainebleau hotel by a mobster known as "The Russian." The modus operandi ended up in the movies thanks to Paul "Skinny" D'Amato, a flamboyant high-roller and one-time prince of Atlantic City nightlife (and the subject of Van Meter's fascinating book) who was privy to the details of the scam and passed them on to his poker pal, *Goldfinger* producer Albert Broccoli.

A similar hustle was also used to steal $500,000 from the famed gambler Nick "the Greek" Dandolos. That game took place poolside at the Flamingo Hotel in Las Vegas and was engineered, according to an article in *American Heritage* magazine, by "a pair of sharps armed with a radio-cue prompter and a telescope."

Prevention and Detection

In recent years, a lot of old-fashioned peeking has gone high-tech. Instead of a partner peering through a hole in the wall, the information is gathered by a miniature video camera concealed in a smoke detector, or snuck up the sleeve of a bystander, and then transmitted to the cheat by his partner via a blinking LED concealed in his watch, or built into a pack of cigarettes lying on the table.

So how do you protect yourself against electronic eavesdropping? The old-fashioned way: Play your cards close to the vest. That means don't pick them off the table, don't bring them up to chest level, don't spread them widely, and don't share them with others. Also, watch where you sit. Is there some point of view— above, below, from the side—where your cards might be seen by another player, or an old lady knitting, or a cunningly placed camera?

And what about the player who answers his cell phone during the game? Is the caller talking about you? Peering at your cards from across the street? The bigger the payoff, the more likely something like this could happen.

THE PORTABLE PEEK STORE

James Swain reports this scam in an appendix to *Deadman's Poker*:

Let's say the game is being played in the lobby of a swank hotel. There are four players. Three are cheaters, the fourth a well-oiled sucker. The cheaters position the sucker so he is sitting in a certain chair. Behind the chair sits a person reading a newspaper. This person is the cheaters' confederate. The newspaper the confederate is reading has a razor slit in its center. By peeking through this slit, the confederate is able to see the sucker's cards. If the sucker were to turn around, he wouldn't see anything wrong.

Now comes the clever part. The confederate signals the sucker's cards to the cheaters by breathing through his nostrils. Short breaths indicate low cards, long breaths high cards. Hustlers call this The Sniff. It's one of the most deceiving ways to signal I know of. For all the sucker knows, the guy behind him has asthma!

36

FALSE SHUFFLING
CONVINCERS—THE BOX
AND THE STRIP

To further razzle-dazzle the marks, or lull them into complacency, a skilled cheat will often *box* and *strip* the deck as part of a false shuffling sequence. A box is simply another name for a cut; usually one third of the cards are shifted from the bottom to the top of the pack, or vice versa. A strip is a series of *running cuts*. One hand holds the deck as the other strips (pulls off) small packets from the top and drops them to the table, inverting their order. When combined with riffle shuffles, these mixing procedures are considered a quick and efficient way to randomize the deck. Every casino has its own version, but all casino dealers are required to riffle shuffle, box, and strip the deck many times each time the cards are mixed.

It should come as no surprise that tricksters have figured out how to mimic these safeguards while actually subverting them. The central artifice involved is a *break*, a small gap in the deck maintained by inserting a bit of flesh from the pad of the thumb or finger. Invisible from almost all angles, the break enables the cheat to box and strip the cards in an apparently random manner while never losing track of the top or bottom portion of the deck. Here's how.

False Riffling and Boxing Sequence   Imagine the cheat has a slug on top of the deck. We pick up the action as he neatly squares the pack following a couple of false riffle shuffles (the 7th Way). The cards are gripped by the long sides, the thumbs stationed at the inner corners, the middle fingers at the outer corners. The right hand begins the box by pulling the lower third of the deck to the right and then diagonally forward, as the left hand lowers its cards to the table. The right hand comes back and ap-

pears to put its cards—which are tilted slightly forward—
squarely on the rest of the pack. The left thumb, however, presses
inward, creating a break, so that the packets never become flush

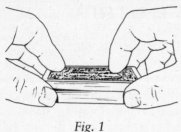

Fig. 1

at the rear (Fig. 1). The two
hands maintain their respective grips on the cards. From
the front everything looks as
it should.

Immediately the cheat
begins another riffle shuffle
by cutting *all of the cards
above the break* to the left.
The packets are riffled to-

gether, ending with the slug from the right hand's packet. The top
is now back on top. The moves are done smoothly, rapidly, and
without hesitation: riffle, riffle, box, riffle, etc. A similar sequence
can be used to control the bottom portion of the pack.

False Stripping Sequence   This sequence, which controls the top stock, begins like the boxing sequence described
above. However, instead of undercutting one third of the deck,
the cheat cuts roughly *four fifths* of the cards to top and holds a
break (this looks identical to Fig. 1, except the top packet would
be thicker). Both hands lift the deck an inch or so above the table
in preparation for the strip. The right hand now assumes full control of the deck, the right thumb taking over the break. The left
hand now begins stripping small packets from the top of the deck
and dropping them to the table. Actually, both hands actually
work in unison; as the left hand takes hold of a few cards, the
hands move away from each other (along the same plane) until
the stripped packet clears the top of the deck. The packet is
dropped to the table and the hands move inward so another
packet can be stripped. After about four or five strips, *all of the
cards above the break are stripped* and added to the tabled pile.
Finally, the right hand, which still holds the original top of the
deck, slaps its cards on top of all to conclude.

There are two ways to control a bottom slug. Some cheats begin by stripping the first packet from the bottom of the deck, fol-

lowed by legitimate strips from the top. This, naturally, keeps the bottom on the bottom and is more deceptive than it sounds. Alternatively, the cheat can preface the strip by cutting the bottom slug to the top, and holding a momentary break beneath it. He then begins the stripping action with *this* packet, once again returning the bottom to the bottom.

A typical, casino-approved shuffling sequence might consist of three or four riffle shuffles, followed by a box, another riffle, a strip, a final riffle shuffle, and a cut. In the hands of an accomplished cheat, a bogus mixing procedure can look exactly the same.

Detection and Prevention

Cheats often hide their manipulative skills by feigning clumsiness with cards. In the above examples, however, the cheat takes a different route and dazzles his victims with a skillful display of card handling that appears to be beyond reproach. How could anything subversive possibly be going on with all that shuffling, cutting, boxing, and stripping? Fairly easily, it turns out. These sequences, when done by a professional, will fool the keenest observer.

So if you can be gulled by a clumsy dealer and snowed by a slick dealer, what's a body to do? Ask the experts, and the advice is always the same. If you have any reason to suspect the cards are being manipulated, shuffle the deck yourself. And always, always watch the cut.

One final tip from expert David Malek. In a casino context, dealers are required to end every shuffling sequence with a one-handed cut. The cards are placed flat on the table and the top half is cut directly onto a cut card, and the cut is completed. This looks exceedingly fair and open. In the cheat's version, everything looks the same, almost. In reality, the cheat maintains his setup on top of the deck and just before the one-handed cut, he cuts a third of the deck from the bottom to the top, and holds a break. Now all of the cards above the break are cut, one-handed, onto the cut card and the cut is completed. What you need to look out for, in other words, is a boxing action followed immediately by a cut. The second cut undoes the first and the stack is back on top.

37

CHEATING AT DRAW— THE ONE-CARD TRANSFER

Five-card draw is a game with an inventory of scams all its own. You can cheat on the deal, cheat on the draw, cheat on the discards, cheat away from the deck, and stack, collude, and "play location" in ways that don't work nearly as well, if at all, in other games. This is partly because each player receives five cards at once, and partly because of the exchange of cards featured in the draw.

Draw became the dominant form of poker in the 1840s, shortly after the size of the deck jumped from 20 cards (10, J, Q, K, A) to 52, and it held that position for more than a century. Cowboys, gunslingers, riverboat gamblers, gold prospectors, railroad workers, and plantation tycoons all played draw. For cheats, the game was a font of inspiration, giving rise to such concepts as holding out (impossible with four players and a 20-card deck), double dealing, double discarding, the spread, the three-card draw trick, and other forms of collusion.

Here we'll look at a versatile technique that enables the cheat to secretly transfer a card from his own hand to his partner's, using the deck as a springboard. It greatly ups the odds that the partner will win the pot, since the card he's given is exactly the one he needs.

The work: The cheats must be seated side by side, the dealer's partner to his left. As the players examine their cards, the cheat's ally, without being obvious about it, holds his cards so that his partner can have a look at them. Let's say he's one card short of a flush, with four diamonds and a club. If the dealer has a diamond, and we'll assume he does, he signals his partner: "Stay in the game—it's on the way." He then palms the diamond in his right hand and drops out, tossing the remaining four cards into the muck as five (see the 30th Way, "Holding Out," for palming details). When it's time to deal the draw, the cheat picks up the deck and transfers it to his left hand, adding the palmed card at the same time. There's no fancy technique: The right hand descends directly onto the deck and adds the palmed card as the pack

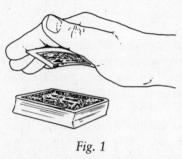

is lifted or slid off the edge of the table onto the waiting left hand (Fig. 1). The cheat's partner draws one and makes the flush. The move is called *capping the deck*.

Fig. 1

Obviously, the transfer can be used to complete a straight, turn a pair into trips, change two pair into a full house, or pass along any valuable card. It works with many styles of palming and can be applied to stud games as well as lowball and other forms of draw.

Some cheating teams to prefer to communicate with signals alone, rather than by exposing the cards.

Prevention and Detection

This is not an easy scam to catch. Over time you may notice that when a certain player deals draw, the guy to his left usually wins. But proving that it's collusion is very difficult, unless you catch the dealer red-handed. And the only way to do that is to grab his wrist en route to the deck and demand to see the palm. If the movies are any indication, this often leads to gunplay. Proceed at your own risk.

38

CHEATING AT DRAW— DOUBLE DEALING

Here are four methods a crooked dealer will use to cop an extra card while dealing. The steals all take place at the same moment—as the cheat deals himself the last card of the round—but each method accomplishes its goal in a unique way.

The Double Deal　In this context, "double dealing" refers to the act of dealing two cards as one. The left thumb pushes over the top two cards in close alignment, using the same mechanics as the second deal, and the right hand deals them as unit. Immediately, the left hand tables the deck and the right hand picks up the cards. There's no time for other players to notice the extra card, and the cards already on the table act as camouflage. The cheat now has six cards when everyone else has five. By double dealing twice on the round, the cheat can start off with seven cards. (See the 30th Way, "Holding Out," for many ways to go from here.) Playing with extra cards is also known as "playing heavy."

The Scoop Addition　Instead of quitting after dealing himself the fifth card of the round, the cheat immediately takes a sixth card and uses it to scoop up his hand, putting down the deck at the same time. Depending on how slippery the table is, the left fingers can act as a stop to aid in the pickup before the deck is placed on the table (Fig. 1).

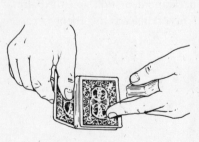

Fig. 1

This is another of those moves that should be obvious

but isn't. As long as the cheat is confident and nonchalant, the ruse is likely to succeed. The move can also be combined with a double deal, to start off with a two-card advantage.

Top Palm Addition   After completing a dealing round, many players transfer the deck from left hand to right before placing it on the table. This is a natural action and draws no attention, which is why a cheat can use the transfer as yet another cover for stealing an extra card. As the right hand takes the pack from the left, the right pinkie pushes forward and down on the top card of the pack, causing it to pop up directly into the palm (Fig. 2). The deck is placed on the table and the right hand drops onto the dealt cards, adding the palmed card. This is known as *capping the hand*. All six cards are slid off the table and brought up to eye level. Some cheats prefer palming the bottom card of the deck into the left hand as the right hand tables the pack. The stolen card is added to the bottom of the hand as the cards are slid off the table.

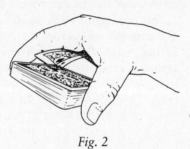

Fig. 2

The Drop Addition   This time the extra card—or multiple cards, if desired—comes from the bottom of the deck. With the pack in dealing position, the cheat secretly riffles the bottom card or two off his right thumb so that the left little finger can hold a break above them. After dealing the last card of the round to himself, the cheat transfers the pack to his right hand, the right thumb taking over the break. The right hand now sides the dealt cards off the table and into the waiting left hand (Fig 3). At that mo-

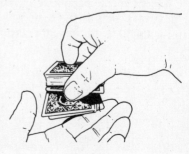

Fig. 3

ment, the right thumb releases the broken cards, adding them to the hand. To the observer, it looks like the right hand flicked the cards into the left and then tabled the deck. This is very deceptive.

Prevention and Detection

These moves succeed because of timing, rhythm, and body language. If the cheat's actions appear natural, the maneuvers pass unnoticed. Moreover, the moves occur at the right moment, as the other players pick up their cards to see what they've been dealt.

Which doesn't mean that the cheat can't be discouraged. One way to reduce the chances of card-copping is to count the deck often—standard procedure in all public card rooms. Another deterrent is to aggressively scrutinize the dealer as he deals. Despite a cultivated appearance of nonchalance, the cheat is always keenly aware of whether his hands are being "burned." The more attention you pay, the less likely it is the cheat will "move."

COPPING AN EXTRA CARD ON THE DRAW

When the muck is nearby, some cheats will wrangle an extra card on the draw by holding out and faking the number of discards. For example, suppose the cheat starts off with a high pair and an ace kicker. He palms the ace, tosses two cards into the muck as three, and lays his pair on the table, calling for "three." The clear display of the two tabled cards must mean three were discarded. Eventually, the cheat cleans up by tossing all six cards into the muck, or by hanging on to the extra card for later use.

THE DOUBLE DISCARD

This gutsy gambit is used when the cheat is dealt a four-card straight or flush before the draw. Say, for example, the cheat holds four hearts and a spade. Most players would play the hand by discarding the spade and drawing one card. The cheat, however, keeps the spade and draws four, placing the discards on the table to his right. If one of the draw cards is the needed heart, the cheat immediately drops it onto the tabled discards and picks up those cards *again,* at the same time tossing the remaining cards aside—*as if they were the discards.* Instead of having one opportunity to make the hand, the cheat has four—and his flush!

The actions make no sense and ought to be obvious to anyone paying attention, yet the ruse works often enough to have been passed down through generations of cheats. Perhaps the discard ritual is so familiar that, when enacted twice, it just doesn't register. When local rules forbid drawing four cards, except to an ace, the double discard can be adapted to work with a three-card draw.

"This maneuver," writes Gerritt M. Evans in *How Gamblers Win,* "requires great adroitness, and discrete advantage players only resort to it now and then . . ."

39

CHEATING AT DRAW—THE THREE-CARD DRAW TRICK

This is another ingenious set of moves from cowboy and river-boat days. The payoff is three of a kind, delivered like a gift from the gods of cheating to the dealer or his partner. The scam is complex, requires two cheats, and takes two complete games to play out, meaning that the gift doesn't arrive until the final cards of the draw round. The method also includes an unusual variable: Neither of the cheats knows which one will get the set until the very end.

Game One The cheats must be seated next to each other, the dealer's partner to his left. During the first game, the dealer drops out. After dealing the draw round, he gathers in the discards, combines them with undealt cards, and culls three of a kind to the bottom of the deck (see the 6th Way, "Culling," for how to do this without attracting too much attention). Let's say they're jacks. He will now position the jacks within the deadwood so that—during the next game—they will arrive at the top of the deck at exactly the right moment for one of the cheats to draw them.

This sounds wickedly difficult but is actually fairly easy. In a six-handed game, for example, the cheat knows that the first round will burn 30 cards. He now guesses that the first four players to draw—the honest ones—will take eight cards among them, bringing the number of burned cards to 38. Therefore, if the jacks are positioned 39th, 40th and 41st from the top of the deck, they will automatically be on top of the deck when the player in the five-seat—the very cheat who is currently stacking the deck—is set to draw. Since 41st from the top is the same as 12th from the bottom, all the cheat has to do is place 11 cards *under* the jacks (52 − 41 = 11) and everything will eventually fall into place. This can be done by peeling the cards singly from the top of the pack into the left hand, then shifting them to the bottom, or by riffling down the outer left corner of the pack with the left thumb, silently counting the cards, then shifting them all in a single cut. When everything is in place, the deck is set on the table and ignored. If other players fold, their cards are added to the top of the stack.

Game Two   To complete the setup the new dealer assembles the deck by placing all of the remaining cards on *top* of his partner's stack. This positions the trips 39th, 40th, and 41st from the top. Following a false shuffle and bogus cut, the cheat deals six hands. This brings the setup 9th, 10th, and 11th from the top. Both cheats remain in the game during the first betting round. Now comes the draw, and the crux of the matter. If the honest players draw eight cards among them as anticipated, the cheat will draw three and get the jacks. But suppose only six cards are drawn? Not a problem. The cheat in the five-seat draws two (making up the difference) and his partner the dealer draws three and wins the prize!

This scam has a lot of leeway. The honest players can draw as few as four and as many as eight cards among them, and the cheats will still be able to steer the ship into port by drawing one, two, three or four cards. And in the unlikely event the stack ends up undealt or in another player's hand, so be it. There's always a next time.

Al Smith, in *Poker to Win,* points out that savvy cheats will often call off this trick when they find themselves against heavy raising in the first round. Although they are likely to win the pot, often with a full house, if anyone thinks twice about it, their play won't add up. Why would someone buck the odds against heavy betting and then draw three? It doesn't make poker sense. Whether the average player would notice this, however, is debatable.

Prevention and Detection

It's up to the dealer to enforce the rules of draw. When dealer and cheat are one and the same, the rest of the players have to keep things honest. The most important rules in draw are first, no toying with the discards, and second, make sure the number of cards drawn equals the number of cards discarded. Personal experience demonstrates that in most home games, neither of these rules is enforced.

Stacks like this three-card draw trick can be wiped out by cutting the deck before the draw. This legitimate safeguard can be requested by any player.

GEORGE DEVOL'S FIVE-CARD DRAW TRICK

From *Forty Years a Gambler on the Mississippi*, by George Devol:

> *I was playing poker once on the steamer* General Quitman. *The party were all full of grape juice. Along about morning the game was reduced to single-handed, and the man I was playing with was fast asleep, so I picked up the deck and took four aces and four kings out, with an odd card to each. I gave him the kings and I took the aces. I gave him a hunch, and told him to wake up and look at his hand. He partly raised his hand, but laid it down again, and I knew he had not seen it. I gave him a push and shook him up pretty lively, and he opened his eyes. I said: "Come, look at your hand, or I will quit." He got a glimpse of it, and I never saw such a change in a man's countenance. He made a dive for his money and said: "I will bet you $100, for I want to show you I am not asleep." I told him I thought he was "bluffing." I said in a joking way: "I will raise you $1,000." So he pulled out his money and laid it on the table, and said: "I will only call you, but I know I have you beat." I showed down four big live aces, and he was awake sure enough after that.*

40

THE SPREAD

Art is not what you see,
but what you make others see.
—Georgia O'Keeffe

Colluders are always putting on a show. They pretend to be honest. They pretend not to know each other. They feign anger and disappointment, friendship and camaraderie, suspicion and surprise. In this morsel of team trickery, the cheats enact a mini drama calculated to cause fellow players to misinterpret what they see and overlook a bold swindle. One cheat gives the other exactly the card he needs to make his hand and nobody notices. The move comes from the heyday of draw poker and, for reasons that will be come apparent, is known as "the spread."

The work: The spread is typically used in this situation: after the draw, cheat A holds a four-card flush—let's say, in spades—plus a meaningless "x" card, and cheat B, his partner, holds a spade that will complete A's flush. There's a lot of money on the table, and many players in the game.

Cheat B sets things in motion by talking trash. He's pissed at how much A has been winning, playing stupidly, getting lucky, taking pots he should have lost—whatever fits the bill. A tells B to shut up and play cards. There's another round of betting and more grumbling. These guys don't like each other very much.

In reality, however, the cheats are following a different script. As they banter, each cheat palms a card: A palms his unwanted "x" card, B palms the needed spade, with the face of the card against the palm. "Flush," declares A as he lays his four-flush on the table, face up, all bunched together. "Let's see 'em," barks B, as he reaches across the table and *adds the palmed card to his partner's hand as he spreads the cards*. It's a flush, all right. A rakes in the pot. B can't believe his rotten luck. Curtain.

To clean up, cheat A adds his palmed card to his victorious hand as he turns the cards facedown and pushes them into the muck. Cheat B concedes defeat and tosses his four cards into the muck without showing them.

Prevention and Detection

The spread is an old-fashioned move that is out of vogue these days. What remains up-to-date, however, is the psychology. The cheats provide a frame of reference that influences the way the other players interpret what they see. Without the show of anger and suspicion, reaching across the table seems fishy. Even if it's not clear what's happening, many would suspect that *something* happened. Add a measure of motivation, and the move flies.

For obvious reasons this play can be run only once a night. Chances of encountering it are slim, and now that you know how it works, it should be easy to spot.

THE SNATCH

Another melodrama of the period uses the same style of dramaturgy to switch a complete poker hand. The cheats call the play when there's a lot of action in the first round and it's clear there's going to be a monster pot.

Cheat A is the main actor. He bets heavily from the start, raising at every opportunity—or at least as much as the opposition will tolerate. On the draw round he has many options: He can stand pat, he can draw one, or he can draw two. None of it matters because the contents of his hand are irrelevant to the scam.

Meanwhile, across the table, his partner cheat B has dropped out of the game and is rabbit-hunting through the discards, putting together the strongest hand he can find—a flush, boat, even four of a kind.

With buckets of cash on the table cheat A is clearly excited, nervous, and impatient, and B's fiddling with the cards is driving him crazy. Finally, he reaches across the table, snatches the cards out of B's hand and slams them onto the table, shouting "What the hell's wrong with you! I've got a lot of money in this game! Stop fooling with the cards!"

This is when the switch occurs. As cheat A reaches for B's cards, he's holding his own cards between the thumb and first finger. These are the cards that are tossed to the table as the cheat grabs his partner's cards between the first and second fingers. It's done in an instant, and cheat A now holds the powerhouse hand he's been pretending to have all along.

41

SHINERS, GLIMS, LIGHTS, AND TWINKLES

Some tricks *are* done with mirrors. In 1552 Gilbert Walker explained how a cheat would seat his victim against a "great looking glass wherein the cheater might always see what cards were in his hand." Few would fall for this ruse today. However, when you shrink the mirror and use it to peek cards *before* they are dealt—the concept works just fine. Cheats call it *playing the lights*.

Hidden in Plain Sight In the cheating trade, any reflective surface used to read cards is known as a *shiner* or *glim*. This ingenious approach utilizes everyday items as reflectors: a polished cigarette lighter, money clip, cell phone, mirrored sunglasses, a cup of black coffee—anything that can be placed on the table without seeming out of place. As the cheat deals, he passes the cards over the shiner, looks down, and remembers the card. The method is out in the open but doesn't register with the other players.

Camouflage In another approach, the gaff remains on the table but the reflector is out of sight, tucked away inside a half-open box of matches, hidden behind a wad of currency, or built into the bowl of a tobacco pipe, or a dummy stack of chips (Fig. 1). This is a clever variation on the theme. Not only is the reflector invisible, it's set at a 45-degree angle, allowing the cheat to read the cards at a greater distance and without having to pass them directly, and sometimes awkwardly, over the gaff. On the other hand, the small size of the mirror means that the cards must be held in precisely the right position to frame the index in the shiner. And, unlike the trusty Zippo, if the gaff is discovered, there's no denying that cheating was afoot.

Despite the drawbacks, this type of shiner was a standard item

WEbster 9-3515 / CHICAGO / K·C CARD CO.

49

GOLD RING SHINER

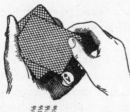

With our Gold Ring Shiner you can read cards as they are being dealt from the deck. Deal a hand and tell every card. Marked cards are not needed. Use any kind of deck. Our ring is made with a highly polished surface so that you can see every card in any kind of light. Looks just like any fine piece of jewelry. Nothing to be hurriedly removed. Simply twist back to normal wear. Note illustration: Ring is best worn on little finger of left hand if you are right handed. We guarantee the fit if you will measure your little finger as listed below.

RING SIZES

To determine the size you need, cut a strip of thick paper so that the ends meet when drawn tightly around the little finger. Then lay one end of the strip at the beginning of the heavy line drawn on diagram and order the size indicated by the other end of the strip.

No. 490. Ring Shiner, Solid Gold . . . . Each **$12.50**

FRENCH MIRROR SHINER

Both our Detachable Shiner and our Palm Shiner are made of finest quality French mirror glass and each is supplied with special adhesive for wearing. Full instructions for use sent with each order. These are most practical made.

No. 491. Detachable Shiner, with Ring Clip to attach to ring . . . . Each **$5.50**
No. 492. Palm Shiner . . . . Each   **4.00**

FRENCH CONVEX SHINER

This is a true CONVEX Shiner specially imported by us to give you a perfect Convex surface for distance reading of cards as they are dealt. Do not confuse this French import with so-called convex shiners which are really concave and not at all practical. This one is exactly as we say and perfect for fast reading.

No. 493. French Convex Shiner . . . . Each **$7.50**

SECRET SHINER

This is one we cannot show a picture of. We know you will like it and will use it, as it is the best in this line. To picture it would give it away.

No. SS-10. Secret Shiner . . . . Each **$10.00**

BILL SHINER

Green in color blending in with your bank roll. Small and compact, making it easy to conceal. Size is supplied for best results.

No. 494. Bill Shiner . . . . Each **$4.00**

MATCH BOX SHINER

Match box is a standard brand box which has a fine mirror inset into one end. Very good results can be had with this device.

No. 459. Match Box Shiner . . . . Each **$3.00**

A deposit of ½ must be sent with all orders.

Fig. 1: A typical assortment of shiners from the K.C. Card catalog, 1961.

in the mail-order cheating business and tens of thousands were sold. There don't seem to be many around these days, except in the hands of collectors.

Handheld Reflectors   Here the shiner is a dime-size convex mirror concealed at the base of the pinkie and ring fingers in the hand that holds the deck. As the cheat deals the top card, he cocks it counterclockwise and inward before pitching it, clockwise, across the table. This action positions the index corner directly over the shiner. The cheat has only to look down and catch his peek. Because the mirror is convex, the image is large, as if seen through a fish-eye lens. This is the method favored by professional glim workers. The peek is surefire and the gimmick can be dropped into the lap between deals. This type of shiner is also known as a *light, flick,* or *twinkle*.

A *cigarette shiner* is a small convex mirror mounted onto a pin and stuck into the end of a filter cigarette. The cigarette is held between the index and middle fingers of the right hand and is positioned slightly below the outer right corner of the deck, preparatory to taking the card for dealing. As the top card is pushed to the right, the index is visible in the shiner. This is a specialty item that the cheat may use only once during a game. As the pot builds and the tension mounts, the cheat lights up and takes his peek.

Prevention and Detection

One way to thwart glim-work is to keep all objects unrelated to the game off the table. No beverages, cell phones, silverware, lighters, or lucky talismans.

Professional cheats use their tools discreetly. A skilled glim-worker won't peek at every card—only those that matter. Sometimes only one player's cards will be targeted. Watch the dealer's eyes as well as his hands.

Finally, be alert to tiny lights that suddenly dance and flicker across the wall or ceiling. This is how the shiner picked up some of its nicknames—from the light and twinkle of a chance reflection.

PLAYING THE LIGHTS IN ATLANTIC CITY

One of the biggest scams ever pulled in Atlantic City involved the use of a shiner. The scammers were a group of Asian gamblers playing high-limit baccarat and betting up to $10,000 a hand—each! In the first casino they hit, they won $1,400,000. They hit another casino the next night for $1,600,000. Cheating consultant George Joseph was brought in to study the surveillance tapes. The scheme was complex, but the key was a bracelet worn by one of the culprits. By simply resting his forearm on the layout, the guy was able to catch a reflection of the top card in the dealing shoe and signal his partners how to bet. By the time this was figured out, the scammers were out of the country.

42

SUBVERTING THE SCRAMBLE

To *scramble* a deck means to mix the cards helter-skelter by swirling them on the table in a circular motion, using both hands. A scramble looks chaotic and disorganized, and it is. But it can also be controlled and manipulated. Under the guise of the scramble, the cheat can cull, flash, and slyly maneuver a stacked hand into position before anyone takes notice.

Positioning a Slug   In the first scenario we pick up the action as the cards are tossed over to the cheat for the upcoming deal. Rather than begin with a riffle shuffle, the cheat starts off with a scramble, creating a disorganized heap in the center of the table. The cheat's partner has tossed over his cards as well, but they lay a little off to the side. This is not by accident. The cards have been memorized so that they can be dealt as known hole cards on the next hand, or used in a location play. After a moment, the cheat "notices" these cards and appears to pitch them into the center of the muck, but what really happens is this: The left hand lifts up on about half the discards, opening them book-

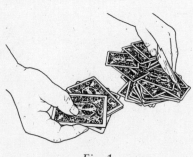

Fig. 1

wise, and the right hand tosses its cards toward the center (Fig. 1). At the very last second, however, the left hand releases its cards, and the slug lands on *top* of the heap, the left hand acting as a backstop. The cheat can now reinforce the illusion by genuinely tossing another clump of cards into the center of the muck. The pack is then squared with the memorized cards on top. It makes no difference that the cheat doesn't know what they are; on the next hand, his partner calls the shots.

In a public card room a scramble is required whenever a new deck is introduced. In this scenario, we'll assume the dealer is crooked and the deck is partially stacked to favor a partner. To scramble the deck yet retain the setup, the dealer skips the required faceup spread and lightly tosses the deck to his left so that the cards slide down the table in an overlapping row until stopped by the waiting left hand (Fig. 2). The right hand now flicks the

Fig. 2: The cards are faceup for clarity.

center section of the spread forward and the left hand scoots its cards back across the table and into the cupped right hand. Both hands swirl the cards around so they get jumbled together, except for the stacked portion which remain under the control of the right hand (Fig. 3). This is usually enough to sell the idea that the cards are mixed. However, in case some skeptical player has kept track of the top of the deck, the cheat adds a convincer by seeming to toss the original

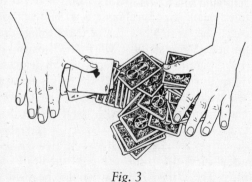

Fig. 3

top cards into the center of muck, using the technique described above.

Culling Cards   To cull cards during a scramble all the action takes place during the squaring procedure. The cards are gathered into an uneven pile and turned on their long side, the faces toward the cheat. Cards are sticking out in all directions and it's easy to spot one or two high ones. As he rotates the cards into alignment, the cheat quickly strips out the target cards and shifts them to the top or bottom. The cull is done rapidly, using whatever valuable cards are at hand. Even if only a single ace is culled, it will provide an advantage in any game.

Flashing   Flashing cards to a partner is automatic. The cheat doesn't have to do anything but square the deck with the faces toward his partner so that a few of the bottom cards can be memorized. By wiggling a few of the cards up and down, the cheat ensures that several are exposed. The cards can be brought to the top of the deck with an overhand shuffle and dealt as hole cards, or retained on the bottom with a false shuffle and cut to the center for a location play, among other options.

Prevention and Detection

Paying attention to what's going on in front of us is something we humans are not especially good at. We're easily distracted and often unable to discriminate between what's important and what isn't. The scramble is one of those things that doesn't seem important. More shuffles will follow, so why pay attention? This makes scrambling subterfuges easy to get away with.

On the other hand, all of the moves are observable. Flashing is self-evident. The culling moves are well covered by the flurry of hand motion that goes with squaring a deck; however, the cheat must look at the deck to spot the valuable cards. Watch the dealer's eyes to catch this. Also be alert for a scramble that leaves a few cards off to the side until the dealer "happens" to notice them. This is the moment when the cheat will toss them to the top of the heap while appearing to chuck them into the center.

43

STACKING THE FLOP
IN HOLD 'EM

This hold 'em scam is remarkable for how much damage can be done with so little work. As the cheat clears the table for the upcoming deal, he flashes the burn cards to his partner: A-7-9. These are tossed into the middle of the deck, which is assembled in apparently haphazard fashion and shuffled—falsely. When the flop is dealt, guess what? A-7-9.

The modus operandi is our old friend the pickup stack (the 11th Way). As the cheat consolidates the deck he positions the burn cards *beneath* all of the original hands. When those cards are dealt again in a different combination, the burn cards automatically appear on the flop. (True, there's a new burn card to be accounted for, but we'll get to it shortly.) The procedure requires no counting or rearranging of cards and works the same way regardless of the number of players in the game.

The work: We pick up the action at the end of a ten-handed game, after the winner has been determined. At this point, there are five groups of cards on the table: (1) the discards from folded hands; (2) the showdown hands; (3) burn cards; (4) five faceup community cards; (5) the rest of the deck. Everything is near the dealer with the exception of the showdown cards.

To set up the stack, the cheat picks up the three facedown burn cards and flashes them to his partner (easiest if the ally is on his right). These cards are used to scoop up the discards and the combined pack is dropped onto the talon. The showdown cards are also corralled and dropped on top of the deck. The burn cards are now beneath the original 20 cards. The cheat picks up the deck, scoops up four of the community cards, and adds them to the *bottom* of the pack. The last community card, which seems to have been left on the table by accident, goes on top. This positions the stack one card deeper and enables a card to be burned without cutting into the setup. Following the requisite false shuffles and cut, the cheat can deal ten hands, burn a card, and the flop will be as anticipated.

Here's another sequence that achieves the same end thanks to a devious use of the cut card to position the stack (see the 33rd Way for other wily uses for the cut card). The conditions are the same, except for the cut card, which lies at the bottom of the talon. Once again, the cheat flashes the burn cards and uses them to scoop up the discards. These are dropped on the table and the talon, including the cut card, is casually tossed on top. The showdown cards are chucked into the center of the pack anywhere *below* the cut card and above the bottom three cards. The community cards can go on the top or bottom of the deck. The cheat now thumbs through the pack, removes the cut card, and places it on the table. At the same time all of the cards below the cut card plus one, are shifted to the top of the deck. The stack is 21 cards from the top and ready to go. The entire procedure seems offhand and thus unpremeditated.

Prevention and Detection

Knowing which cards will hit the flop doesn't guarantee victory but it sure saves money. Obviously, the cheat doesn't need to *pay* to see the flop since he already knows what it is.

Although the setup is a snap, the scam actually requires a high level of skill—in particular, a convincing full-deck false shuffle (see the 49th Way). A partial false overhand shuffle might work when attention is lax, but an overhand shuffle should be taboo in the first place.

In a crooked gaming establishment with a skilled mechanic as the house dealer, this scheme can be played many times a night. The best protection is constant vigilance and a legitimate cut.

44

CUTTING CLASS—FOUR FALSE CUTS

Cheats use false cuts to enhance the apparent fairness of false shuffles and to maintain the deck in order as it is seemingly cut prior to the deal. Many of the techniques are simple, but in the context of a game the following operations will fool anyone.

A False Cut from the Hands   This pseudo cut can follow any in-the-hands false shuffle. With the deck in dealing position, the left thumb levers the pack away from the palm, so that the right thumb and fingers can grasp the lower half of the pack. These cards are stripped out and slapped to the table. (Fig. 1 shows the start of the strip-out.) Immediately the right hand returns for the remaining cards and slaps them onto the tabled cards. The illusion of a genuine cut is extremely convincing. In fact, if the cheat slides the deck in front of the cutter for the official cut, he may "knuckle the deck" and waive it off. Big mistake.

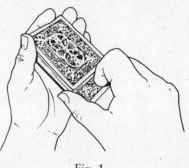

Fig. 1

A Triple False Cut from the Hands   Try this with deck in hand and you may fool yourself. Cut the deck into three packets by cutting off one third, followed by another third and then the balance of the deck. The packets are placed on the table in a row in A-B-C order. The right hand now picks up A and places it on B, picks up the combined AB, slaps it onto C, and returns the deck to the left hand. The sequence has the feeling of inverting the order of the deck when, in fact, everything is in the original order. A confident attitude and a brisk, snappy rhythm go a long way to sell the move.

Hustler's Triple Cut   This is the type of false cut a skilled card handler will toss into a flurry of false table riffle shuffles. The pack begins on the table, gripped at both ends. The right thumb and middle fingers slide out the bottom two thirds of the pack and cut it to the top, but stepped to the left about half an inch. The right thumb and fingers adjust to grip both the upper and lower packets. (In Fig. 2, the left hand has been removed for clarity, but would actually mask the stepped condition from the front.) Now

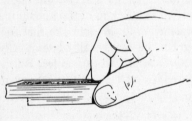

Fig. 2

the left thumb and middle finger grasp the lower half of the top packet. The right hand moves to the right, taking with it *everything but* the cards held by the left hand. The left hand drops its cards onto the table. The right hand comes back directly over the tabled packet. The left thumb and fingers take the top packet of the right hand's cards and drops them on the tabled packet as the right hand moves away. The right hand now returns and slaps its packet on top to complete the sequence.

This is less complicated than it sounds. The right hand does all the moving as the left fingers grip the proper packets. Done smoothly, everything flows. There are many variations of this type of cut. This one comes from *The Annotated Erdnase*, Darwin Ortiz's illuminating commentary on *The Expert at the Card Table*.

Tabled False Cut—I   This counterfeit cut is used by the cheat's partner to fake the obligatory cut. The pack is gripped by the corners between the thumbs and middle fingers. The right hand strips out the *bottom* half of the deck, moves forward and upward about four inches or so, and slaps the cards onto the table. As part of the choreography, the right hand also tilts outward slightly, briefly exposing the bottom card to those seated across the table. Immediately the right hand returns for the remaining cards—the original top half of the deck—and slaps them onto the first packet to conclude. This is very bold, but it works. When performed briskly, it is impossible to tell that the cutter has pulled out the bottom half of the deck rather than the top. The flash of the bottom card greatly adds to the illusion. If desired, the cheat can complete the cut rather than the cutter.

Tabled False Cut—II   This cut is even more audacious than the previous one. The cheat simply cuts off the *top* half of the deck and puts it back on top. What makes it deceptive is the cheat's attitude plus a couple of misdirective touches. The hands grip the deck exactly as above. The right hand briskly pulls the top half of the deck forward, upward, and inward, slapping it back onto the bottom section. Rather than being lifted directly, however, *the bottom card of the top half* is scraped across *the top card of the bottom half* as it is pulled forward. This helps create the illusion that the bottom half is being stripped out. Sometimes the cutter will begin the action by looking away from the deck, and then return his gaze to the pack as he completes the cut. This focuses attention on the final action, the apparent completion of the cut. The move is called a *scrape cut*.

Another false cut commonly used by the cheat's partner is the *slip cut*, which is explained in the 7th Way, "False Riffle Shuffles."

Prevention and Detection

Even when you know what to look for, all of these false cuts are deceptive. Often the only tell is the briskness and bravado the cheat incorporates into the cut in order to "sell" the move. If you can't determine where the packets are coming from, ask the cutter to slow down. Better still, use a cut card and insist that the deck is cut slowly and with one hand. Or cut the cards yourself.

45

THE ONE-HANDED
TABLE HOP

This nifty sleight appears to complete a genuine cut when it does nothing of the kind. The fact that it is done one-handed makes it very deceptive under the right circumstances.

The work: The move relies on speed and snappy execution. The cheat begins by tabling the deck to his right. The cutter cuts the top portion to the left, and the cheat reaches across the top portion and picks up the bottom half of the deck, wedging the long side of the packet into the fork of the thumb (Fig. 1). The right hand now glides inward over the original top portion of the deck. The right

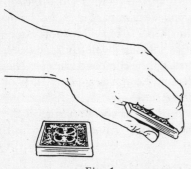

Fig. 1

fingers extend, contact the outer long side of this packet, and begin sliding it inward along the table. The thumb-clipped cards remain firmly in place. It should appear as though the right hand's cards are about to be dropped on top of the lower packet; however, during the sliding action the packets are transposed.

The right wrist flexes so as to bring the outer side of the clipped packet into contact with the table directly behind the original top half of the deck (Fig. 2). At the same time the right fingers snap the tabled packet inward and on *top* of the clipped packet, which acts as a ramp. The move occurs in a split second and the continuous motion of the right hand obscures the maneuver. The packets are squeezed together, lifted from the table, and transferred to the left hand for dealing. The look of the move is

that the bottom half of the
deck is added to the top half
as the pack is slid inward;
nothing more than that.

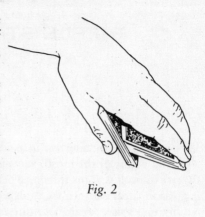

Depending on how the
deck is cut and where the
packets lie, the cheat may
begin by sliding the bottom
portion off the edge of the
table and directly into the
fork of the thumb. The hand
then returns for the top portion of the deck, completing
the move as above.

Fig. 2

The sleight is easier to do on a baize-covered table than on a
slippery surface, such as bare wood, but it can be done almost
anywhere.

Prevention and Detection

Once you know it exists, the one-handed table hop is easy to
recognize. The tell is the speed of the move as the cards are
scooped and swept from the table.

However, this is a sleight the cheat will use only occasionally
and only when attention is lax. It's especially effective in a heads-
up game with an opponent seated directly opposite. The cheat
will make eye contact as he performs the hop, shifting attention
away from the cards at exactly the right moment.

The more you focus on the deck, the less likely a cheat will act.

46

RIFFLE STACKING

Stacking, or "running up," a hand under the guise of riffle shuffling is one of the most exacting forms of card-table artifice. What's difficult isn't the technique per se—which consists of inserting spacer cards between the cards to be stacked—but doing so invisibly, under fire. An amateur can stack one or two cards and fool an unsuspecting player. Anything more requires an extraordinary level of skill that, fortunately for the rest of us, few cheats possess.

The work: In most riffle-stacking scenarios, the first step is to cull the requisite cards to the top of the deck. The pack is then split and the cards are interlaced in a highly controlled fashion. The more players in the game the more difficult the procedure.

We'll begin with a simple example: stacking a single ace to fall to the dealer in a four-handed game. The top half of the deck is split to the right and the packets riffled together so that when the right hand runs out of cards, the left hand has exactly three cards remaining. These are released on top of the ace, producing the desired arrangement: x-x-x-A. This is easy to do deceptively with practice. The left thumb learns the *feel* of three cards, and the cheat has no need to look at the deck.

With two aces, things become trickier. Now the speed of the riffles must be timed so that the left hand ends up with three "x" cards at the same moment the right hand has control of the two aces (Fig. 1). Then the cards are released alternately, one from the right, three from the left, one from the right, producing the arrangement:

Fig. 1

A-x-x-x-A. If the cheat has a partner in the one-seat (often known as the cheat-seat) the stack would be ready to roll. To deal the pair to himself, the cheat shuffles again, adding three positioning cards to the top of the stack.

Now we'll leap to a four-card stack. Although no cheat in his right mind would deal himself four aces, the method is what we're interested in. As usual, the aces begin on top of the deck, which is split to the right to start the shuffle. Now the cheat must synchronize the riffles so that that last seven cards fall like this: one from the right hand, three from the left, and three from the right, yielding the arrangement: A-x-x-x-A-A-A. The sequence is repeated three more times to insert spacers above *each* of the remaining aces. Doing this in slow-motion is easy. The hard part is doing it at normal speed, by feel alone, without looking at the deck, without slowing down, without inserting too few or too many spacers, and while appearing benignly indifferent to the proceedings.

Consider stacking a seven-hand game and things get mind-boggling. Six spacers would have to be slipped between *each* target card without missing a beat. To avoid this impossible scenario, advanced riffle stacking is always a team effort. For example, if the cheat's partner plays a stud hand to the river and folds with a pair of unexposed kings, he sends them over for the next deal with five spacers already in place. Other partners do the same. Adjustments are made by the mechanic as he shuffles. With coordinated team play and expert signaling, this combination of cull stacking (the 11th Way) and riffle stacking allows the cheat to run up one or two strong hands in very short order.

While there are other approaches to riffle stacking, such as starting with the culled cards on the *bottom* of the deck, I'll limit myself to one more method known as the "perfect shuffle." When the deck is divided exactly in half, and the packets shuffled together so that the cards alternate perfectly, every card in the deck doubles its numerical position. After one perfect shuffle, the cards that were in positions 1, 2, 3, 4, 5, move to positions 2, 4, 6, 8, and 10. After a second perfect shuffle, those same cards migrate to positions 4, 8, 12, 16, and 20. This mathematical certainty has serious repercussions for cheating. It means, among other things, that the top five cards on the deck can be stacked to fall to the dealer in a heads-up game, in exactly one shuffle! That's an instant flush, straight, boat—whatever the cheat culled to the top of the deck as he cleared the board—stacked in exactly one shuffle! In a four-handed game, the same result takes two shuffles. Nor does the shuffle have to be entirely "perfect" in this scenario: As long as the top 20 cards interlace perfectly, it works.

Entire books have been devoted to the perfect shuffle and its permutations and ramifications, all of them beyond our scope here. Suffice it to say that it is the most expeditious way to insert spacer cards in many situations. The principle is a relatively new one. It was first mentioned by Victor Innis in *The Inner Secrets of Crooked Card Players* (1915). The shuffle is also known as the *faro*, *butt* and *weave* shuffle.

Prevention and Detection

The two major tells in riffle stacking are hesitation and staring at the deck. Hesitation occurs as the cheat makes last-minute adjustments to the timing of the riffles, and as he begins to consciously alternate the cards. Staring happens simultaneously, as the cheat *visually* confirms that each hand controls the correct number of cards. This is something even experts do when the stack is complex. Watch the dealer's eyes for a moment of intense focus on the deck.

Another tip-off is a curious pause that may occur *before* each shuffle. As the cheat goes to split the deck, the hands momentarily freeze. It looks as if nothing is happening but, in fact, the cheat has angled up the top half of the pack along the inner long side, and is imperceptibly riffling spacer cards off the right thumb onto the left. When the deck is cut for the shuffle, the left hand already has control of the spacers, slightly separated from the rest of the packet. This streamlines things later on; however, the *time* the cheat must take to get ready is a blatant tell, if you know what you're looking at.

The tell on the perfect shuffle is that, in most executions, the cards aren't actually riffled off the thumbs. Instead, the ends of the packets are butted together and the cards interlace automatically as the result of just the right pressures. This is very difficult to do and unlikely to show up at your weekly game.

47

PAPERING THE NEIGHBORHOOD

Have your own cards, and if others send out to buy cards, let them buy from men you can trust. Examine them inside and out and edgewise; touch the corners; if they are rough, or too smooth, or hard, or uneven, do not play; for before you can recognize what is wrong, your opponents will perhaps ruin you.
—Girolamo Cardano (1501–1576),
Book on Games of Chance

On June 15, 1895, the *Fort Wayne News* ran this story about a far-reaching scam:

A gang of sharpers with their headquarters in this city is practicing one of the cleverest swindling games that has been devised for many a day. Their operations extend over the states of Ohio, Indiana, Kentucky, Illinois and West Virginia. The scheme has at its foundation marked cards. A member of the gang first enters a town representing himself to be a salesman for a playing card company. He visits all places where cards are sold in the vicinity, selling his stock of marked cards at a price that is next to nothing under the pretext of "introducing the goods." For days the unsuspecting innocents are bled and cheated. The strangers can send out and buy cards that read so well there is no suspicion. After the town is successfully worked they follow up their advance man and play the game all over again. It is said that at Indianapolis the gang cleared over $15,000 [roughly $1,750,000 today] in a few weeks.

Of all the methods for slipping a marked deck into play, this one wins my vote as the most diabolical. Every store in town sells nothing but marked cards. What a concept!

The scam is known as *papering the neighborhood* (*paper* being a term for marked cards). It's still done today, albeit in a slimmed-down version that targets one high-stakes game and one nearby retail outlet, ideally a late-night convenience store. The day before the game, the hustler hits the store and buys every deck of cards, except for one or two. The next day he returns and clandestinely restocks the shelves with the same cards which, in the interim, he has unboxed, marked, and resealed, with the bar codes, price tags, and rack hangers intact (see the 20th Way, "Skinning the Deck"). On his way out he buys the remaining unmarked decks. If the cards are kept behind the counter, the cheat buys all the red-backed decks on day one and returns them on day two, explaining that he had intended to buy blue-backed cards, or jumbo index cards, or pinochle decks. He shows his receipt, the clerk obligingly makes the switch, and the scammer leaves the store with an inventory of marked decks.

Scene two. The game is under way, the cheat is at the table, and the marked cards are still in the store. What next? In many versions of the tale, the cheat waits until the witching hour and then destroys the cards in play. He spills beer on them. He rips them up in a conniption fit. He secretly bends them and then complains that they're bent. One way or another, he ruins the cards. The timing is such that it's too early to break up the game and too late to buy a new deck anywhere but at the Kwiki-Mart with the marked decks. The cheat is too upset or too drunk to drive, so someone else does the deed. And the tide turns.

Two big-league mobsters, Bugsy Siegel and Arnold Rothstein, were apparently ripped off by this scam. Siegel got taken by a small-time hustler named Jimmy Altman in the $100,000 buy-in game Siegel ran at the Flamingo Hotel in Las Vegas. In *Poker Nation*, Andy Bellin tells us that Altman used three confederates: One bought all the cards in the Flamingo's gift shop, another complained that the shop had no cards, and the third, masquerading as a card salesman, restocked the store with marked decks. To get the paper into play, Altman expressed displeasure with the cards in use, claiming they might be marked. A gofer was dispatched to the gift shop for a deck more to his liking. Siegel lost nearly a million dollars.

Arnold Rothstein was not so fortunate. After dropping $322,000 in a three-day poker marathon in a Manhattan hotel, Rothstein refused to pay up, claiming that the cards—which had been purchased at a cigar stand in the lobby—were marked. A month later Rothstein was lured to another hotel by the game's disgruntled host, George "Hump" McManus, and shot. Rothstein died the next day, refusing to name the shooter, and McManus was acquitted for lack of evidence.

Prevention and Detection

This is a multilayered and far-sighted scam. In some ways, it's related to the classic confidence games in which hustlers fabricate a highly detailed and realistic "big store," like the fake horse parlor in *The Sting*. All to take down one victim. In this case, the "big store" happens to be a real one, but it serves the same purpose: winning the mark's confidence. After he's been cleaned out, the chump never considers marked cards because he knows their source.

So how paranoid should you be? Are the decks at the 7-Eleven marked? Is your game the target? Unlikely, if the stakes are small. But cheats, it should be clear by now, will go to any length for a big payoff. If you play cards for serious money, you should carefully inspect every new deck that comes into play.

48

THE COOLER

The cooler is a stacked deck designed to win *all* the money in one fell swoop. It accomplishes this by lavishing certain players with seemingly bulletproof hands—flushes, full boats, even fours of a kind—while reserving the best hand for the cheat. Switched with the deck in play in the blink of an eye, the cooler infects the marks like a virus, causing delusions of invulnerability, euphoria, belligerence, and betting fever. These symptoms soon give way to shock and despair as the promise of imminent victory is wrested away. In the end there's only one survivor: the cheat. That all this delirium can be programmed into a deck of cards and kept in a pocket until showtime is rather remarkable.

There are two parts to the cooler scam: preparing the deck and switching it into play.

The Setup   Arranging a cooler is a bit like running a movie backward. Once the cheat knows the parameters of the script—how many players, what the game is, where the marks will sit, who is to win the pot—he storyboards it by laying out all the cards in their final positions: the four sixes that win, the kings full and ace-high flush that lose, along with all the other cards to be dealt and folded.

Then he collects the cards in reverse order, starting with the last card dealt and moving counterclockwise in a circle, placing each card facedown on top of the other, until all the hands are assembled. The remaining cards go underneath and the cooler is set. If the cheat doesn't have all his information in advance, he may show up at the party with several coolers, each set for a different number of players.

Draw poker is the classic cooler game. In Hollywood, the

cooler is usually stacked to take down a single player (Nicolas Cage in *Honeymoon in Vegas*, Jamie Foxx in *Shade*). The mark gets a pat hand, bets the ranch, and bites the dust. But the cooler can be set to lure in many players at once as long as the targeted players—and the cheat—get their pat hands before the draw. That way, if anyone deviates from the script by dropping out or staying in unexpectedly during the draw round, it doesn't affect the outcome of the game. (In a stud setup, the cooler must also be arranged to prevent unexpected plays from derailing the scam. The more confederates at the table, the easier it is to make sure this doesn't happen.)

In a hold 'em scenario, a cooler has the unique ability to improve each of the suckers' hands at the same time. For example, a ten-handed game might target three players with A-A, K-K, and J-Q. A flop of A-K-10 gives the marks trip aces, trip kings, and an ace-high straight. A second 10 on the river cements the deal with aces full, kings full, and the straight. And who wins? The cheat, with four tens.

The intriguing thing about this scam is that there seems to be a lot of freedom in the game, but none of it matters. Any of the ten players can check, bet, raise, call, fold, or go "all in," and the outcome will be the same. The four 10s win. (A hold 'em stack is assembled like a draw cooler: Everything is laid out and picked up in reverse order, starting with the river card, followed by a burn card, the turn card, another burn card, the flop, etc.)

The Switch   This is the more challenging part of the exercise. How do you exchange decks midstream without anyone noticing? As usual, there are many approaches. The switch can be made with the aid of a third party, known as a *switchman*. This might be a waiter who comes around with a tray of drinks, the cooler hidden beneath it, and makes the exchange with the cheat as the drinks are served (good for games in hotels and cruise ships). In a public card room, the corrupt dealer can start off with the cooler as his second deck. When it's time for a new deck, he simply brings out the cooler, false-shuffles, false-cuts, and deals (for a full-deck false shuffle see the 49th Way). In a home game in which two decks are alternated (one red, one blue), the cheat's partner can make the exchange when it's his turn to shuffle. Often, however, the switch is done by the cheat himself, immediately after the deck in play has been legitimately shuffled and cut. Gerritt M. Evans explains a classic method in *How Gamblers Win*:

> *There are several old-fashioned ways of making the substitution such as dropping a bill on the floor and bringing up the "cold deck" after stooping as if to search for the money, etc. But these methods are clumsy. The artistic way of doing the thing is to raise the prepared pack from the lap to nearly the line of the table in the left hand, and when the true pack is cut, to draw the latter to the edge of the table with the right hand directly over the "cold deck," which at that instant is brought to the surface; the discarded pack being simultaneously dropped into the lap where a spread handkerchief is ready to receive it.* [Later, the handkerchief is wrapped around the deck and pocketed.]

The keys to making such moves invisible are timing, misdirection, and a concept known as *splashing* or *building in*. This simply means that *every* time the cheat picks up the deck after the cut, he does so by sliding it off the table into his waiting left hand. He does this again and again, all night long—without switching anything—until the actions are so familiar that they pass unnoticed—and then he switches.

But usually not without additional cover. A split second before the switch, the cheat's partner knocks over a stack of chips, or sneezes hilariously, or reaches into the pot to make change. Attention immediately shifts to the partner, if only for a second, and the switch is made. This crucial moment of distraction is known as the *turn*.

The modus operandi is virtually the same when cold-decking the sucker on his own deal. This is the most powerful application of the cold deck concept. The cheat sits to the dealer's right, the cooler in his lap. When the deck is offered for the cut, the cheat's partner "turns" the dealer, and the cheat cuts the deck, completes the cut, and makes the switch as described above. This is the swindle that bamboozles the mob-boss runner Larry Jennings (Jamie Foxx) in *Shade.* Jennings deals himself an intoxicating four 10s, bets a horse-choking bankroll that isn't his, and is wiped out by four jacks. Because he was the dealer, the idea of a swindle never occurs.

For obvious reasons, the cooler is played only once during a game, and almost always late in the evening, when players are less attentive and more likely to risk all on what seems like a cinch hand. The cooler also gives the cheat the luxury of playing honestly all night, then cleaning up in one hit. The cooler, incidentally, gets its moniker from the actual temperature of the cards. Waiting off stage until ready to administer the *coup de grace,* the deck is said to be literally cooler than the cards in play.

Cold decks are also known as "ice" or "bombs."

Prevention and Detection

You won't see the switch, you won't notice the turn, and you won't feel the change in temperature as the cooler slides into the game. What you can't fail to notice, however, is the explosion of cash piling up on the table as the chum hits the water.

Is it a cooler? Is it luck? Is there a way to tell the difference? Probably not until it's too late. There is, however, one sure way to avoid being wiped out in one fell swoop. Fold 'em instead of hold 'em. When? When you're dealt a pat hand in a high-stakes game with strangers; when betting limits are removed and your cards seem unbeatable; when it's the last hand of the night, everyone's in, and you've got a monster hand.

Some things are too good to be true.

49

A FULL-DECK FALSE SHUFFLE

The first time I saw a full-deck false shuffle, I was convinced it was some kind of trick deck. There was no way to genuinely riffle shuffle the cards together, square the deck, and not change the location of a single card.

Well, I was wrong. Not only *is* there a way, there are many ways. The one we'll consider here—a classic gambler's method—is known as the *push-through shuffle*. The name comes from the central action of the sleight. As the shuffled packets are telescoped together, one packet is pushed *through* the other and emerges from the rear of the deck, unseen. Then the packets are stripped apart and reassembled in their original order. Cheats use the move when they want to apparently shuffle a cooler, or when working with a deep stack that goes down 20 cards or more. In the right hands, this shuffle is as convincing as you can get.

The work: The deck begins in standard riffle shuffle position with the two packets flat on the table in shallow V-shape formation. The riffling action commences with the right-hand packet and ends with the left, the cards riffling off the thumbs at an even rate. The packets are straightened and telescoped into each other about three quarters of the way. (In Fig. 1 the top card has been turned faceup for clarity.) It's at this point that the deception begins.

Precise finger positions are important. The pads of the fourth fingers are posted on the outer corners of their respective pack. The other fingers lie naturally along either side, and the thumbs rest on the inner side of the packets, near the center. The packets

Fig. 1

are now pushed together. From this point on all the work is done by the right hand; the left simply keeps its packet anchored in place. As the right hand moves toward the left, the ring finger, which is doing all of the pushing, swivels outward and then in again, describing a small counterclockwise arc. This causes the right-hand pack to move diagonally into and partially *through* the left half. The left thumb eases off the inner side of the pack to allow this to happen. (In Fig. 2, the left hand has been removed for clarity.)

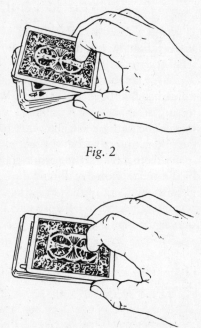

Fig. 2

The packets are now brought back into alignment along the same plane. The thumbs and fingers squeeze the deck from opposite sides. This causes the long sides to become flush, but at the same time the original right-hand packet automatically becomes side-jogged from the left side of the other packet. (In Fig. 3, the left hand has been removed for clarity.) This condition is hidden by the left-hand fingers at the front end of the deck. The observer assumes that the deck is flush on all sides.

Fig. 3

Now the packets are stripped apart. The left hand remains stationary, holding the side-jogged packet between the thumb and middle finger. The right hand, mirroring the left, pulls its packet smartly to the right and diagonally forward and slaps it onto the table. It then comes back for the rest of the deck and places these cards on top. These actions appear to be a simple cut. In a variation, the left hand can strip out its cards and place them directly on top of the right hand's packet, again simulating a cut. The sequence is performed fluidly with one action blending into the next. The shuffle is usually repeated.

Please keep in mind that the above description is only one of dozens and dozens of potential variations. With the requisite skill, timing, and rhythm, an accomplished cheat can fool even hustlers who are familiar with the concept.

Prevention and Detection

From a defensive point of view the most important thing to know about a full-deck false shuffle is that it can be done. Chances are, when you see it, you won't "see" it.

There are, however, a few potential tells. One is that a "cut" immediately follows each shuffle. When several shuffles are done in succession, anyone acquainted with the push-through will recognize the pattern. On the other hand, the cheat may forgo the cut and go directly from the strip-out into another shuffle.

Two other tells are the result of poor technique. If the cards are held too tightly they will bind during the strip-out, leaving stragglers sticking out of the left packet. Also, some cheats permit the remaining packet to collapse like an accordion during the strip-out, as the interlaced cards are pulled out.

RESOURCES

The full-deck false shuffle is one of the rare instances in which sleight-of-hand moves created by card magicians have been adapted by cheats. Usually, it's the other way around. In truth, most magicians' sleights have little relevance to card cheating, although they can be used to give the *appearance* of advanced sharping skills in a performance setting.

Two noteworthy masterpieces of false shuffling invented by magicians are the *Zarrow shuffle*, invented by the beloved amateur magician Herb Zarrow, and the *Heinstein shuffle*, an ultraconvincing in-the-hands false riffle shuffle created by Karl Hein. Both shuffles are explained by their creators on teaching DVDs marketed to the magic community.

50

DECK SWITCHES

A deck switch is a deceptive maneuver used to exchange a marked deck or cooler with the deck in play. We looked at a classic sleight-of-hand method in the 48th Way, "The Cooler." The following approaches rely more on timing and an understanding of what will and will not register with observers at the table.

The Chair Switch   The cheat makes the switch as he pulls his chair closer to the table. Everyone recognizes the actions: The hands grab on to opposite sides of the chair seat, the body "bounces up," and the chair is scooched forward. The cheat does this with deck in hand, and in the process exchanges one deck for the other.

Exactly how this is engineered depends on the chair and the sightlines, but basically the marked deck—and this works only with a marked deck, not a cooler—is taken from a side jacket pocket and jammed under either thigh shortly before the switch is to be made. Both hands go out of sight at the same time; the house deck is dropped into the lap (sometimes onto a spread handkerchief), the other deck is grabbed and the chair scooted in. Both hands come back up at the same time, and the house deck stays where it is until the cheat can pocket it at an opportune moment.

Sounds tricky, but the whole sequence is invisible because the switch occurs in the downtime between games. The cheat gathers in the cards, pulls in his chair, shuffles, and deals. Attention doesn't focus on the dealer until the shuffling begins, and by then the switch is over. Try using the same switch to ring in a cooler (which *can't* be genuinely shuffled) and what you get is this: The cheat gathers in the cards, shuffles, allows the cut, pulls in his chair (making the switch), and deals. The sequence now draws attention to the moment when the deck goes out of sight, rather than glossing over it. It just doesn't work. Which is why some unheralded cheat invented the jacket switch.

The Jacket Switch   This requires a special shirt and jacket. The shirt has an extra pocket, about 2 inches deep and about 2½ inches wide, located under the right armpit. The cooler fits into this pocket and protrudes halfway out, so that it can be easily removed without fumbling.

The jacket has a large baggy pocket sewn into the inner right side, at around waist level. The edge of the pocket is pinned to the shirt or otherwise hooked up so that at the crucial moment, the mouth of the pocket will open automatically, as explained below.

The switch is made a beat or two *after* the deck has been shuffled and cut. The cheat holds the pack in dealing position in his left hand. However, before sailing the first card, the cheat reaches across his body with his right hand to snuff out a cigar in the ashtray located, not by chance, at his left elbow. The choreography here is very specific: As the right hand crosses left, the left hand moves close the chest and the torso leans forward as well as to the left. This causes the right side of the jacket to shift to the left and completely screen the left hand. At that moment the cheat drops the house deck into the baggy pocket and takes the cooler. The left hand barely moves: The dropped deck automatically falls into the pocket and the cooler virtually presents itself to the left fingers. As the right hand returns to the right, the jacket also shifts right, revealing the left hand looking exactly as it did a moment before. Nothing seems to have changed. The move requires precise timing as well as expert tailoring.

Prevention and Detection

These switches are difficult to spot. The actions that make them possible are logical, motivated, and apparently unrelated to possible deception. If nothing seems out of the ordinary, nothing registers.

A worthwhile exercise, even if cheating is not suspected, is to try to focus on the deck from the moment the dealer gets the cards until the winner is decided. This will often reveal many vulnerabilities in the game, such as accidentally or deliberately flashed cards, moments when the deck disappears from view, and misassembled cuts. Maintaining concentration is not easy. A typical friendly game is filled with distractions as well as the effects of beer and booze.

A marked deck, it's worth noting, is switched in early in the game whereas the cooler is a late-night special.

I'VE BEEN CHEATIN' ON THE RAILROAD . . .

This deck switch comes from the short-lived era of railroad hustlers. Train crews were generally less tolerant of cheaters than were the riverboat captains who got a piece of the action. The era lasted long enough, however, to produce this clever exchange.

The cheats typically set up their game in a club car, next to a window. When it was time to ring in the cooler, one of the cheats would light up a cigar, work up a sizable stem of ash, and then accidentally scatter ashes all over the table and the cards. To clean up, he'd scoop up the mess and hold everything out the window so that the wind could blow away the ashes. In reality, everything was tossed out the window, including the entire deck. When the cheat brought his hands back in, they were holding a different deck taken from a sleeve, a secret pocket, or wherever he had the foresight and skill to conceal it.

51

THE SHIFT—AKA HOPPING THE CUT

So far we've looked at the cheat's four favorite methods for overcoming the pesky problem of the cut:

1. Ignore it and deal.
2. Rely on a partner to cut at a crimp, brief, or bridge.
3. Rely on an unsuspecting player to cut at a crimp or bridge.
4. Reassemble the deck in the original order in the act of completing the cut.

To these approaches we add one last method known as *the shift* or *hopping the cut*. Most likely developed by card sharps of the sixteenth century, the shift is used to undo a completed cut. As the pack is squared, the original order is instantly restored.

The work: We pick up the action as the cheat completes a cut by placing the bottom half of the deck onto the original top, but stepped slightly to the left. The pack is immediately transferred to the left hand. The stepped orientation is hidden by the back of the

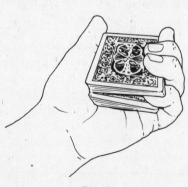

Fig. 1

right hand, and the motion of the deck ensures that nothing out of the ordinary is noticed.

As soon as the pack hits the left hand two things happen. The left little finger enters the deck between the two halves of the deck—the shelf makes this easy to do—and the pack is squared. This is the starting position for the shift. (In Fig. 1, the right hand has been omitted for clarity.)

Under cover of the right hand, the left fingers now draw the top half of the deck to the right—gripped between the middle and ring fingers on top and the little finger below—and pivot it into a perpendicular position (Fig. 2).

At the same time, the right thumb and finger pull *up* on the lower packet. As soon as the edges of the packets clear each other, the left fingers curl in, and the left hand's cards are snapped into position on the bottom of the deck, restoring the pack to its original order. The move is done in a split second.

Fig. 2

This is, admittedly, a bare-bones description of an exceedingly difficult sleight. Erdnase, who considered the move useful for card conjuring, but a "last resort" at the card table, worked out several versions, none of which pleased him. "The shift has yet to be invented," he concedes, "that can be executed by a movement as coincident card-table routine." In other words, there is no way to perform the actions in a way that appears completely natural within in the context of the game. However, when circumstances demand the move, Erdnase offered this advice: "The resourceful professional failing to improve the method changes the moment; and by this expedient overcomes the principal obstacle in the way of accomplishing the action unobserved."

In Erdnase's era, when draw poker and five-card stud where the games of choice, "changing the moment" meant postponing the shift until after dealing the first round. In draw, for example, the cheat would start with, say, three kings on the bottom of the deck. After the cut he would hold a break while dealing and perform the shift as the other players picked up their cards. The kings would then be dealt from the bottom on the draw. As Erdnase points out, "The shift can be made with a much more natural action when about to lay down the deck than when picking it up, and also because the deck is much smaller after the deal and therefore much easier to shift."

Cheats have also devised a number of one-handed shifts which, although infrequently used, are workable in the right context. The easiest of these—which the reader can master in a short time, just for the fun of it—is the *Charlier shift*, named for the shadowy magician and card sharp who taught it to a few British magicians before he mysteriously disappeared in 1884.

The pack is held at a 45-degree angle at the tips of the left fingers, with the ring and middle fingers on one long side, the thumb on the opposite side, the pinkie at the inner end, and the index finger curled beneath the pack. The thumb now relaxes its hold on the lower half of the deck, causing it to drop onto the palm (Fig. 3). The pad of the index finger now pushes upward on the bottom packet until it con-

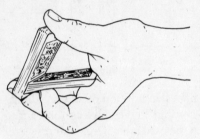

Fig. 3

tacts the thumb (Fig. 4). The fingers extend slightly so that the packets clear each other. The original top packet now rests on the curled index finger (Fig. 5). The index finger now gently slides along the bottom of the packet and joins the other fingers on the

Fig. 4

long side of the pack, and the thumb gently pushes downward. This causes the packets to coalesce and fall onto the palm.

As a magician's flourish, the move is done openly as a one-handed cut. For cheating purposes, cover is provided by the back of the right hand, which fully extends over the deck to square the short ends between the thumb and fingers. The shift is executed and the right hand completes the action of squaring the deck.

The Charlier shift can be used when the cutter fails to cut at a bridge or crimp. The cheat completes the cut and transfers the deck to the left hand. In the first action of the shift, the deck will automatically fall open at the crimp, allowing the pack to be restored to its original condition.

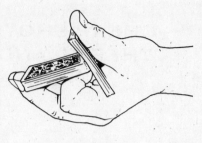

Fig. 5

Detection and Prevention

Even with a masterfully executed shift, it is usually possible to tell that "something" has happened, though exactly what may be unclear. Any awkwardness, unusual turns of the hands or body, or out-of-place gestures, can indicate a shift. The more closely you watch the dealer, the less likely he is to move. Conversely, when players are distracted and the game is easygoing, even a mediocre shift will fly.

RESOURCES

The shift is one of the bedrock moves of card magic, where it is more often called the *pass*. Instructions can be found in *Expert Card Technique* (Hugard and Braue); *The Expert at the Card Table* (Erdnase); and *Card College* (Giobbi). For a visual tutorial on DVD try Richard Kaufman's *On the Pass*, and Ken Krenzel's *The Pass*. Both teach many variations of the sleight, none of them easy.

52

CHEAP SHOTS—TRAPS, THEFTS, AND ALTERED APPEARANCES

This is a mixed bag of cheap tricks—a collection of low and weaselly deceits that don't merit individual chapters of their own. They all occur away from the deck and involve no technical or ethical skills. Some may not even qualify as cheating.

Appearances

Praying "Oh, Lordie, send me a king," implores the cheat when, in fact, he has no need for a king. If the prayer is answered, the cheat is perceived as having made his hand when, actually, he may have nothing. If no king appears, he's seen as having missed the hand when, in fact, he may already have made it. Often used to give the appearance of catching a straight or flush, it's all smoke and mirrors.

The Hole-Card Flip The cheat manipulates the perceived strength of his hand by switching a board card with a hole card. The up-card is simply placed flush on the pocket card and the two are turned over as a unit. Maybe deuces are wild and the cheat has a deuce showing. A card or two later, when attention is focused on another hand, he flips the deuce for a neutral card and hopes no one notices. Amazingly, they may not. Likewise, a pair on the board can be undone with a simple flip. These swindles need a really loose game.

Four-Flushing The cheat deliberately misdeclares the value of his hand. "Ace high flush," he says, laying down four hearts, perhaps with a bit of diamond index peeking out from beneath. If no one calls him on it, and the declared hand wins the pot, the cheat rakes it in and buries the evidence in the discards. If caught, he worms and squirms his way out of it, pleading the lateness of the hour, too much beer, or an honest mistake. The same trick is done with an almost straight.

The Ambiguous Hi-Lo The moment of truth in home-style hi-lo comes when each player extends a fist and declares whether he is going "low," "high," or "both ways," by opening his hand to reveal zero, one, or two chips. The cheat puts a chip in one hand, nothing in the other, and rests both hands near the center of the table. Then he waits for everyone else to declare before opening the hand that gives him the best outcome. The ruse is transparent, but it takes a gutsy player to ask "What's in the other hand?" when the first is shown empty.

Traps

Checking Out of Turn The point is to lure the early seats into the game by pretending to have a weak hand while actually holding the nuts. For example, the cheat is in fourth position. Position one checks and the cheat checks. When informed he was out of turn, he apologizes. Meanwhile, seats two and three bet or raise based on the cheat's check, and are sandbagged.

Raising Out of Turn A bet is made and the cheat comes in with a hefty raise—but out of turn. He apologizes and play backs up to include the bypassed players, but they fold, anticipating the raise. The cheat has gotten rid of one or two players and maybe steals the pot with nothing.

Hiding The cheat plays possum in a late position with a killer hand. He pushes his cards off to the side or barricades them behind a stack of chips. He looks away and pays no attention to what the other players do. The competition forgets he's there. When the others commit, he springs back to life and raises.

Thefts

Shorting the Pot   Petty cheats will take advantage of the curious fact that some players do not clearly remember if they just anted up or not. So the cheat doesn't ante and claims he has. Often, another player will make up the difference, if only to keep the game moving.

Playing Light   In friendly games, if a player runs short of chips during a hand, he's often allowed to "play light." Instead of putting money *into* the pot, he bets, calls, or raises by drawing chips *out of* the pot. The "light" chips represent the amount the player will owe to the eventual winner of the pot, if he doesn't win it himself.

There are several ways to scam the system. The cheat may keep the lights in a messy pile close to the pot. That way, if he drops out early in the game, there's a chance the lights will be perceived as part of the pot, and the debt they represent overlooked. Conversely, the cheat may keep the lights in a neat stack close to home. If he drops out, he will buy more chips and stack them next to the lights, hoping they all blend together. If nobody mentions the lights, neither does he. Finally, and most audaciously, the cheat may play light until he accumulates a stack, then start betting from the stack of lights! When nailed, he will tap-dance his way out of trouble (insert your own excuses here).

Prevention and Detection

Problems can be avoided by following card-room rules. Ante in turn, bet in turn (scold the miscreants who get only one more chance), and no playing light. If a miscaller cannot see what cards he's holding, he should be sent home for his own good. In hi-lo games, there should be no ambiguity about which hand is making the declaration. If you don't know, ask.

Conclusion

Many have said that there is no such thing as a friendly game of poker. Not so. For millions of players the game is about camaraderie, bonding, and deepening friendships over a weekly game, played for dollars or quarters, with rules that ensure that nobody gets scorched. It's a wonderful institution, and I salute it.

Put a big pile of cash on the table and things change. Greed kicks in and the trickster goes to work. It's a fact of nature. But now that you know about strippers and shiners, paper and paint, crimps and jogs, you're a lot safer, aren't you? Absolutely! And can you still be cheated blind and left clueless? Absolutely! It's in the nature of things to trust appearances. We are easily fooled, even by something we know, when it comes at us unexpectedly and from a different angle.

Many of the protection tips in this book apply to a range of scams and can be easily summarized: watch the dealer, cut the cards deliberately, begin every game with a new deck, change decks frequently, buy quality brands, count the cards from time to time, keep the discards off limits, play your cards close to the vest, and know who you're playing with. More can be said, but I'll leave the last words to Erdnase.

> There is one way by which absolute protection against unknown advantages may be assured, that is by never playing for money.

> The player who believes he cannot be deceived is in great danger. The knowledge that no one is safe is his best protection.

> In offering this book to the public the writer uses no sophistry as an excuse for its existence. . . . It will not make the innocent vicious, or transform the pastime player into a professional; or make the fool wise, or curtail the annual crop of suckers; but whatever the result may be, if it sells it will accomplish the primary motive of the author, as he needs the money.

Bibliography

Asbury, Herbert. *Sucker's Progress*. 1938. Reprint, New York: Thunder's Mouth Press, 2003.

Austin, Jake, ed. *A Friendly Game of Poker*. Chicago: Chicago Review Press, Inc., 2003.

Bell, J. Bowyer. *Cheating: Deception in War & Magic, Games & Sports, Sex & Religion, Business & Con Games, Politics & Espionage, Art & Science*. New York: St. Martin's Press, 1982.

Ben, David. *Dai Vernon: A Biography*. Chicago: Squash Publishing, 2006.

Britland, David, and Gazzo (Gary Osborne). *Phantoms of the Card Table*. New York: Thunder's Mouth Press, 2004.

Charles, Kirk, and Boris Wild. *Hidden in Plain Sight—A Manual for Marked Cards*. Chicago: Fun Incorporated, 2005.

Devol, George. *Forty Years a Gambler on the Mississippi*. 1877. Reprint, Austin: Steck-Vaughn Co, 1967.

Erdnase, S. W. *The Expert at the Card Table*. 1902. Reprint, New York: The Conjuring Arts Resource Center, 2007.

Edwards, Charles. *Perfecting Your Card Memory*. New York: Exposition Press, 1963.

Evans, Gerritt. *How Gamblers Win*. New York: G. M. Evans, 1865.

Fabian, Ann. *Card Sharps, Dream Books, & Bucket Shops*. Ithaca and London: Cornell University Press, 1990.

Forte, Steve. *Casino Game Protection*. Las Vegas: SLF Publishing LLC, 2004.

Forte, Steve. *Poker Protection*. Las Vegas: SLF Publishing LLC, 2006.

Garcia, Frank. *Marked Cards and Loaded Dice.* New York: Bramhall House, 1962.

Hicks, Jim, ed. *The Gamblers.* Alexandria, VA: Time-Life Books, 1978.

Ireland, Laurie. *Lessons in Dishonesty.* Chicago: Magic, Inc., 1938.

Johnson, Karl. *The Magician and the Cardsharp.* New York: Henry Holt and Co., 2005.

Joseph, George. *The 101 Most Asked Questions About Las Vegas and Casino Gambling.* Las Vegas: Atiyeh Publishing Group, 1996.

Kinney, Arthur, ed. *Rogues, Vagabonds & Sturdy Beggars.* Amherst: The University of Massachusetts Press, 1990.

Livingston, A. D. *Catching Poker Cheats.* 1973. Reprint, Guilford, CT: The Lyons Press, 2005.

Marcus, Richard. *Dirty Poker.* City: Undercover Publishing, 2006.

Maskelyne, John Nevil. *Sharps and Flats.* 1894. Reprint, Las Vegas: GBC Press.

Maurer, David. *The Big Con.* 1940. Reprint, New York: Anchor Books, 1999.

Meyer, Joseph. *Protection.* 1909. Reprint, Las Vegas: Mead Publishing Company, 1999.

Ore, Oystein. *Cardano the Gambling Scholar.* 1953. Reprint, New York: Dover Publications, 1965.

Ortiz, Darwin. *Gambling Scams.* New York: Dodd, Mead & Co., Inc., 1984.

Ortiz, Darwin. *The Annotated Erdnase.* Pasadena, CA: Mike Caveney's Magic Words, 1991.

Parlett, David. *The Oxford Guide to Card Games.* Oxford, England; New York: Oxford University Press, 1990.

Radner, Sidney. *How to Spot Card Sharps and their Methods.* New York: Key Publishing Company, 1957.

Robert-Houdin, Jean Eugene. *Card Sharpers—Their Tricks Exposed or the Art of Always Winning.* 1861. Reprint, Las Vegas, NV: GBC Press, 1983.

Scarne, John. *Scarne on Cards*. 1949. Reprint, New York: Signet, 1973.

Smith, Al. *Poker to Win*. 1931 Reprint, Las Vegas, NV: GBC Press, 1975.

Wiesenberg, Michael. *Free Money—How to Win in the Cardrooms of California*. Secaucus, NJ: Lyle Stuart, 1984.

Wolfe, David, and Tom Rodgers, eds. *The Puzzlers' Tribute*. Natick, Mass: AK Peters, Ltd., 2002.

Videos and DVDs

Forte, Steve. *Steve Forte's Gambling Protection Series* (video) Vols. 1, 2, 3.

Joseph, George, *Cheating at Poker* (DVD)

Malek, David. *Cheating at Hold 'Em—The Essentials* (DVD)

Piacente, Sal. *Poker Cheats Exposed* (DVD).

Turner, Richard. *The Cheat* (DVD).